FIND 'em
GET 'em
KEEP 'em^{SM}

Brian E. Butler

Outskirts Press, Inc.
http://www.outskirtspress.com

ISBN: 978-1-4787-7138-8

PRINTED IN THE UNITED STATES OF AMERICA

Dedication

To everyone who has ever sold anything for a living.
A noble profession.

Acknowledgements

With gratitude to all the teachers I have had on these subjects and all the customers with whom we tried, failed and ultimately shared success. With appreciation for all the cassette and CD programs, seminars and books I have learned from. With thanks to all my co-workers who have put up with me when I get on my "soapbox" about these subjects.

Table of Contents

Introduction

At one point in time for over a decade my wife and I had at least one child in the house under the age of two. Eight kids in eleven years will do that to you. It meant countless joy with all of the first steps, first words and laugh-a-minute interaction between brothers and sisters.

It also meant, just as obviously, many a sleepless night. Countless midnight feedings, trips to the bathroom and 2:00 a.m. drinks of water will cause you to lose more than a few winks.

But even more than that are two things that used to keep me up, but don't any longer. For as I came to realize that much of the "kid" stuff was *out* of my control, I finally came to understand how much the "business" stuff was *in* my control.

It's never been and never will be perfect. Things change constantly. Technology and competition are always pushing you to find new answers and more value for your customers. But I've found that by following certain principles, I don't lose anywhere near as much sleep as I used to about losing existing customers or not finding enough new ones. Not that there are many good reasons for either. Both having good customers leave or having a great potential one not come on board can really increase your antacid intake and your insomnia.

Without finding, getting, and keeping enough of the *right* customers and clients for your business in the long-term, nothing else will much matter. I don't believe in the "customer is always right" philosophy, but rather, you *must* always have the *right* customers for your business to survive and thrive. You might have the best business plan, cutting edge production equipment and the most talented employees. But without a steady stream of repeat customers and a steady stream of new "converts," your business is bound to wither and die. Customers are why businesses are *in* business.

For the purposes of this book, Finding 'Em is all about the marketing effort, Getting 'Em discusses the selling process, and Keeping 'Em details customer service strategies. Like a finely-tuned orchestra, your organization will "sing" when all three work in harmony.

Many organizations have success in one or two areas but rarely all three. When you can align your efforts in all three areas with an intense focus on satisfying the customer, you can have many restful nights and no worries except wondering how to spend the money.

Like many organizations, perhaps you're finding it harder than ever to get enough chances to win new business. The buyer/seller relationship has become very complex. It can be like an elaborate game of hide and seek. To win that game, you must first Find 'Em. If you'd like to have and hold on to more of the right customers, read on………

1
Find 'Em

"The aim of marketing is to know and understand the customer so well the product or service fits him and sells itself"

Peter Drucker

The ultimate goal of marketing is to Attract customers by making yourself attractive to them.

Marketing is everything you do to promote your business, from the second you dream about it through the time you actually have customers buy your products and services. It encompasses all aspects, from naming and branding your company, through the ways you present your value proposition to your target audience. Peter Drucker, the acknowledged leading management authority of the 20th century, said that marketing and innovation were the 1st concern of all businesses, more important than anything else including finances.

As cliché as it sounds, good marketing is not an expense but rather an investment. Most successful companies, even ones that had a unique market position at the start, eventually have to differentiate themselves from the competition. The only way to do this in both the short term and long run is marketing.

Today marketing consists of the original big four: price, product, place and promotion, but now also includes people, productivity, process and physical evidence.

Done correctly, effective marketing will;

- Achieve all growth and revenue goals
- Communicate a consistent message about your company
- Influence customers and potential customers to buy
- Focus on customer needs
- Control the perceptions of the marketplace toward your company, product and service

- Convey the desired value proposition of your offering
- Allow for "top of mind consciousness" of your target audience
- Educate your customers and prospects as to solutions to their problems
- Communicate your expertise in a specific area
- Speak to customers' problems and your solution

Good marketing is the catalyst of continuous customer acquisition.

1. The A – B – Cs of Marketing

Unlike accounting, production or other business processes that have a repeatable "right" way, marketing has sometimes been more art than science, beholden only to the results of the effort rather than how "proper" the approach. Marketing of your product or service will have, however, some consistent themes that will increase the likelihood of success. To get the desired result, effective marketing will:

Attract the attention of your desired target market
Begin to influence the prospect's decision-making process

<u>C</u>ommunicate a low-risk, easy next step action toward buying

A - In love beauty may be in the eye of the beholder; but in business attractiveness is in the eyes of the customer. Is the packaging of your product attractive? Is the appearance of your store pleasing to your potential clientele? What perception does your literature and advertising give to both your prospects and customers?

Even *more* importantly, how and where do you attract the customers you are really looking for – the <u>right</u> ones? (More on that later).

The goal is to *differentiate* yourself from the competition in meaningful ways that are **relevant** to your target audience.

B - Educate people about how to make the correct buying decisions. Make sure to give them all the information they request or need in order to be able to make the purchasing decision for your product or service.

There are three primary reasons why businesses buy things. To increase revenue. To decrease costs. To improve efficiency. You want those things for your business and your prospects want them for theirs. Consumers may buy for pleasure, ease, status or function. But everyone buys for his or her own reasons, part emotionally and part logically.

People want to feel like they've made the best buying decision possible. Arm your potential customers with information that will help guide them through the purchasing process. By giving prospective customers the most information about the **K**ey **B**uying **F**actors (KBF), you will begin to build a higher **P**erceived **L**evel of **C**redibility (PLC). All things being equal, a consumer will almost always go with the person or people they trust the most. Providing the most information goes hand-in-hand with building the most trust.

If as a marketer, you can determine the "hot buttons" (KBF) of each individual prospect, educate them as to what the best deal for them is, and offer <u>proof</u> that you provide the best deal in terms of **value**, you win!

C – It's unlikely to be able to fit all the things someone needs to make a buying decision into one ad or direct mail piece. And most items above a certain price point are not an impulse purchase but rather contain an investigative *process* that leads to a buy / no buy decision. Understanding each prospect's **unique** Decision Making System (DMS) is key to ultimately making a sale.

If you can learn what the typical steps in your prospect's DMS are, you have a chance to guide the process to the conclusion you want – a sale for you.

Do your prospects need;

- A free report or white paper
- A customer testimonial or referral
- A free sample
- A test drive or similar product test
- A site visit
- A discount coupon
- A visit from a sales representative

Whatever it is they need, make sure you offer the easy, no-risk next step as a way to keep the process moving forward.

2. It's Not About You

Most marketing fails for one simple reason. Whether advertisements, product brochures or general conversation, too many people and companies think buying decisions are made by "showing and telling" all the wonderful things your product and service can do. Yawn. We are all overwhelmed with claims of newer, faster and better services by almost everyone. The problem is this does nothing to make a product stand out or speak at all to what is important to the customer.

For marketing to be truly effective, the focus must be on satisfying latent customer needs. Product "pushers" reinforce stereotypes that salespeople in general can't be trusted. When the focus is concentrated on the customer, marketing stops focusing on the *act of selling* and instead taps into their *reasons for buying*. Too often marketing has asked customers to behave in ways that run exactly opposite to what they feel is in their best interests.

In its most pure form, good marketing asks (then answers) the question – "What can we do to help?"

In my area there is a regional modern day version of the old five and dime called Benneys. Thought to be obsolete when the Wal-Marts starting coming to town, they have not only survived but prospered. Why? Because they are conveniently located. They are easy to get in and out of. Since their merchandise is somewhat limited you can still quickly find what you need. They have a knowledgeable salesperson to greet you who can, not only show you where the item you're looking for is, but also assist in explaining things to you. All and all – this is an excellent example of helping customers.

From the customer's perspective there are three questions to ask yourself to see if you are on the right track marketing wise.

1. *What's in it for me?* Customers might initially notice clever or loud advertisements or campaigns but in the long run they will be turned off if there is no payoff for them.

2. *So What?* Can you pass this test? If you promote things like fifty years in business or tout a certain certification, you may be opening the door for prospects to ask this question.

3. *Can I get the same thing somewhere else?* Look at your brochures and ads. Think about your competitors for a minute. Is your sales content pretty much the same as theirs? If your literature says basically the same thing your competition does, you've done nothing to differentiate your product or service. If you can't

show the differences – your customers may check elsewhere.

When answering the question "what can we do to help?" it forces a deeper level of analysis that will focus your attention on the customer--where it belongs.

3. A Recipe for Success

Every great meal has a recipe that helps it turn out the way the chef intended. If he or she is satisfied with it, while they may "tweak" it over time to produce subtle changes in the appearance or taste, they are able to repeat the success again and again.

In business disciplines such as accounting or a manufacturing production line, there are processes that are repeated over and over again to generate a consistent result. Marketing, in and of itself, has no easily transferable "recipes" because success is a moving target governed by almost infinite choices for customers and ever-changing market conditions.

But to ensure a more consistent "top-line" performance there is one recipe that will move your program in the right direction most of the time.

Think of it as a "vowel-based" system to greater marketing success; A-E-I-O-U.

Attract – **E**xcite – **I**nform – **O**ffer – **U**nderstand

Attract. As we've already said, the 1st goal of marketing is to attract potential customers to your product and service. In this country we literally see thousands of messages a year through commercials, billboards, advertisements and the like. The sad truth is that a very small percentage of them actually interrupt our attention and leave any impression. No attraction, no attention, no sale.

Excite: Our attention span in this immediate-gratification world is growing shorter and shorter. As marketers, even if we have created something that initially grabs a prospect's attention, if we don't intrigue and excite them right away, they will lose interest in seconds. People gravitate to sporting events, casinos and theme parks because of the excitement value. You must excite people about using your product quickly to remain in consideration for their business.

Inform: Trust and doubt are two of the key buying factors in the purchase decision for just about anything. By being seen as expert in your field, the organization dispensing the most information to prospective customers, you help gain credibility (trust) and eliminate doubt (fear). Here is where you attempt to define the criteria of a good purchase and effectively build your case that you have the best value.

Offer: Ask and you shall receive. Maybe you've heard of the concept. In the sales part of the equation, it's called asking for the order, closing the deal. In the marketing phase, it's getting the next step, advancing one base. Rather than trying to "push" a sale you're trying to "pull" a customer through the buying process. Low risk offers, free trial, free white paper, 'join our mailing list' etc., all are easy ways to keep your prospective customers within your ability to influence (ATI) them.

Understand: You can't market to, sell or service what you don't know. The more information you can gain as to each prospect's unique decision-making system (DMS), the more feedback you get as to your perceived level of credibility (PLC), the more of their key buying factors (KBF) you know and how well you maintain your overall ability to influence (ATI) them over time will dramatically improve your chances of winning the right customers.

4. Don't bring a fishing pole to catch butterflies

One of the most dangerous decisions that a company or organization can make is to think that *everyone* is a good customer. There might be a few exceptions but the general rule is to stay with what you're already good at, or focusing on the specific problems you tend to solve is a far better bet for customer satisfaction and long-term success. We don't go to the general practitioner for a foot problem but rather a podiatrist. For heart problems we see a cardiologist and for skin issues, a dermatologist. In today's ultra-competitive world, specialization rules.

In much the same way, when you go to market you must know what the unique value structure of your organization is in relation to your customers' needs.

In a book written by Michael Treacy and Fred Wiersema titled, *The Discipline of Market Leaders*, the authors discuss the three basic ways to organize your mission. The three options are operational excellence, product leadership or customer intimacy.

Operational excellence means providing dependable products at good prices with great convenience (Think Wal-Mart). One-to-one relationships with customers are not highly valued because processes are stream-lined and standardized and transactional efficiency is prized. Operationally excellent companies tend to offer less variety and follow rigid business plans.

Product leaders are at the cutting edge of innovation (Think Bose). They take advantage of all ideas whether internal or external, get to market fast or 1st and make their own products obsolete in favor of new ones. Product leaders are passionate about quantum leaps forward and "hitting it big" with one new idea.

Customer-intimate companies focus on serving the needs of specific customers (Think Nordstrom). They are very concerned with the lifetime value of a client over many years of loyal buying. Deep knowledge of buyers' likes, dislikes, buying cycles, patterns, and trends that may influence them is critical to the success of these organizations.

Know what you are, who you're trying to attract, and what tool to bring to catch the right customer.

5. Have a game plan before game day

Around the Boston area the last few years we have

had a relatively successful football team called the New England Patriots. Winning three Super Bowls in four years gains both some respect and some scrutiny. When experts analyze the reasons for these exceptional results, one thing comes up again and again. The Patriots usually have a better strategy, a better *game plan*, than their opponent on any given Sunday.

In marketing, it is important to have a precise strategy, and then the proper tactical execution, in order to win the game. Most studies still indicate it takes at least five to seven contacts to make an impression with a prospect and turn him or her into a customer. A detailed marketing plan allows you to build a successful process to help convert these prospects in an efficient and productive manner.

A sound marketing plan will help accomplish three important things.

1. <u>Save time and money</u>. A carefully-thought-through plan will help you anticipate other needs such as collateral. By thinking about all features, benefits and target markets ahead of time, you can limit "reinventing the wheel" by reusing key text and graphics.

By making an assessment of the current target markets for your product and services, you will limit the wasted effort chasing prospects that would not buy despite any number and variety of attempts. Focusing your efforts on those most likely to buy (MLB) will pay off with faster and larger revenue streams.

2. <u>Build your brand</u>. Because it's so difficult to have your business development efforts rest solely on the backs of the sales force, a well-rounded plan must incorporate many elements that communicate the consistency of your message. The negative price of an inconsistent message is seen in confused and/or indifferent customers.

A brand is much more than a logo or a slogan. It includes the pervasive values you want to communicate in the marketplace. All of your marketing, whether print, email, web, radio or TV campaigns should be designed to leave no doubt in your prospects' minds that they are all from your company. A plan that builds your brand will help consistently communicate all your positive attributes.

3. <u>Measure results</u>. All too often creative marketing ends there--just being creative. It might win some design awards but not deliver any impact to the top line. The goal of any marketing plan must be to see an increase in revenue. Design your efforts so that results can be measured objectively, not subjectively.

    With technology you are able to track open rates and click through rates to your website for email campaigns. Direct mail marketing that includes a response card can help you measure the percentage of people interested in your offer. Redemption coupons offer you the ability to learn which customers take advantage of such programs. A winning marketing plan will anticipate all these things and take advantage of pushing the right buttons for you to generate superior results.

6. Test the Waters before diving in

The most famous competitive archer of all time was a man named Howard Hill. His claims to fame include many hunting records and an astonishing record in tournaments. At one stretch, Howard Hill entered, and won, an amazing 196 archery tournaments in a row. Imagine, if you will, even the great Tiger Woods winning 19 golf tournaments in a row, never mind 196. Impossible you'd say and I'd agree.

The reason Howard Hill won so often is readily apparent. He hit the target, specifically the bull's-eye, with greater precision and regularity than the other archers. How similar it is to business and marketing where the organizations that can hit their target audience with greater regularity and precision "win" the game, and earn the dollars. There aren't too many awards given out for shooting a shotgun. Focus, precision and execution comprise the winning combination.

The key to knowing your target is research. As my faculty advisor reminded me (constantly) during my final project for my MBA, it's called *exhaustive* research for a reason. Having some idea of who will buy from you is good. Doing some research about your prospective customers is better. Knowing who will buy from you and why is best. "Build it and they will come" may have worked for Kevin Costner in the movie *Field of Dreams* but is not a healthy recipe for success in marketing and selling your company.

There are several ways to get the best data possible on your target market, be they customers or prospects, to ensure a good strategy will be followed up with the proper execution in order to get results.

1. <u>Survey your current customers</u>. This could be done via phone, personal interview, email or direct mail. It will help in many ways. First, it will show them your genuine interest (sincerity is a must) in their opinions about your product and service and how it helps them (hopefully). Secondly, it may provide you with some "low-hanging" fruit. The law of taking things for granted probably means you've overlooked some problems that your customers have that you haven't asked about but could solve for them. Learning about them here should lead to more sales. Third, it will improve your sales effort because surveys are all about questions and, knowing what to ask and look for, will help your sales team do their job better. Fourth, it can supply senior management insight into whether or not the proposed marketing and business strategies are resonating in the marketplace. Fifth, you should "stay ahead of the curve" and be able to learn about the goals and trends that are affecting your customer. Sixth, a well-designed survey that gets responses should increase the loyalty of the customers who took the time to respond.

And seventh, you should be able to better aim at your prospects by knowing what is important to your current customers, assuming you want more of the same.

2. <u>Buy Lists</u>. In the information age, Big Brother really does know a lot about us. The sophistication and depth of information that is available is staggering and can be put to good use. The ability to acquire lists and target by SIC Code, demographic, socioeconomic, and psychographic information allows marketers to get to their desired audience. Since mass marketing is all but extinct, mass customization is the way to reach specific niches and individuals in order to get your message heard.

3. <u>Conduct Focus Groups</u>. Whether prospects, customers or both, this type of meeting handled by an experienced professional can lead to a treasure trove of information through which you can make wise decisions. It can be extremely valuable and gives you the green light to go, the yellow light to proceed with caution or the red light to stop.

4. <u>Online bi-directional requests for info</u>. As we'll discuss in a bit, you can now build a response tracking component into your direct mail campaigns where targeted individuals can respond and provide both feedback and additional information on a *personal* web site designed just for them.

These and other tools are just some of the ways that can help you aim at the right target. Test the waters before you get in over your head. It's the careful swimmer who makes it to shore safely.

7. Make a Big Splash and lots of Ripples

Realize the odds are not in your favor. Chances are, depending on your product and industry, there are probably at least a dozen or in some cases multiple dozens of companies you would consider competitors vying for the same business you are. The failure rate for startups remains over 90%. And because of the impact of technology and globalization, existing companies face an increasing set of challenges to remaining a reasonable business option for their customers.

If you are starting up a new business, entering a new market, launching a new product, or re-creating yourself, it is vital to "cut through the clutter" and announce your offer to the world in a way that will actually get people's attention. While the tactical execution of each situation remains different based on what the strategic marketing goals are, consider all the following tools and saturate your message in as many as possible that are appropriate. Options include:

- Television
- Radio
- Magazines and Trade journals
- Newspapers
- Classified ads
- Direct Mail
- Email
- Fax blasts
- Telemarketing
- Web sites
- Signs and Billboards
- Flyers and door hangers
- Yellow pages and similar directory listings
- Co-op advertising opportunities
- White papers
- Audio and video messages on cassette, DVD, or CD

- "30 Second" Commercials for Sales Reps
- Educational seminars
- Point-of-Purchase Displays
- Printed Collateral like business cards and brochures
- On-hold messages
- Open houses
- Free trials or samples

Like when we were kids throwing rocks into the water looking for the big splash, go for the same effect with your "go to market" effort.

<u>Nurture</u>. Now that you've gotten some attention the first time, you need to sustain it to have potential customers become actual. As we've mentioned, studies still show that it takes 5-7 times for someone to recognize the company and associate the products and services that go with it. Unless your timing is exceptionally perfect (unlikely), not enough folks will be looking for what you have at exactly the moment you first get their attention. More likely, they will consider you over time and evaluate your offer against what they are currently doing or buying as they come to know you.

Often referred to as "top-of-mind conscientiousness," it is your ability to be thought of at the time when a customer is making a buying decision that is often the difference between getting and not getting the business. Design your follow up communication to be "pleasantly persistent," not so often as to overwhelm but not so infrequent as to show a lack of interest.

If you have established a permission-based database, you could send;

- Emails
- Postcards
- Small promotional products with your company logo
- Product samples
- Occasional phone call
- Newsletter
- Invitations
- Surveys
- Special offers

Your tactical execution must include this component to ultimately be successful. Don't be fooled into thinking that just because you have a great idea, product, service and campaign you've discovered the "silver bullet" and will become a quick success. Odds are, it will take time. And nurturing your target audience over time to get them to convert their purchases to you is an essential part of the plan.

The big splash may get the necessary attention, but it is the constant ripples on the shore that will wear down the rocks and get the most results over time.

8. Make it Personal

Think about the ways companies try to sell you. How much attention do you give a direct mail piece that starts out "Dear Occupant"? Or even worse, "resident." I don't know about you but I am truly not impressed when an organization buys a list and begins a sales letter with Dear First – Middle Initial – Last Name. As you notice billboards, commercials and point of purchase displays of all kinds, do they speak to you and your particular interests?

With businesses and organizations of all sizes and shapes discovering it more and more difficult to find customers (and for non-profits – donors), the only way is to make your appeal exceptionally **relevant** to your prospect. Many experts say mass marketing is dead, replaced by mass *customization*. Savvy marketers can now reach each potential prospect with a totally customized, individually targeted message.

In the landmark book, *The One to One Future*, by Don Peppers and Martha Rogers, the concept of one-to-one marketing is explained as the ability to interact with potential customers, find out what is of importance to each one, and customize your message and offering to them individually.

Using what's referred to as cross-media or multi-channel marketing, you can "surround" your prospects with your tailored message. Some of the features and advantages of this kind of marketing include:

- Relevancy. Perhaps in this day and age, there is no more important concept for marketers than that of being relevant to your target audience. We all "tune out" the noise of advertising to some degree. By speaking to what you *know* is important to each prospect, you greatly increase your chances of winning a customer today--and for life.
- Brand and campaign consistency. After designing and sending a direct marketing piece, you can now follow it up with an email that has the same graphics and offer as the mailed literature. By backing that up with a telephone campaign, you can increase your variety and number of attention-getting attempts.
- Two-way communication. Technology now gives you the ability to interact with your prospects

in a dynamic manner. How would you like to offer each individual prospect of your service a personalized web site just for them to come visit and learn more about what you can do for them? And link that page to your web site. This is 100% possible and doable. Need to verify and/or gather more information to make your database even more powerful? Can do. Building a two-way dialogue increases both your perceived level of credibility (PLC) and your ability to influence (ATI) for the immediate sale and long-term relationship with each customer.

What you can now do is "swap" both text and graphics and produce truly *one-off* brochures and offers to each prospect. Take for instance a college or university that would like to portray their school as the "right fit" for each prospective student. Based on what information the soon-to-be high school graduates' put on their common application, each institution of higher learning could glean from that the "key buying factors" (KBF) of each person, and present to them the features they are looking for that <u>match</u> the strengths of the school. If Sue wanted a school that had a good computer department, had an active athletic department and was near the water, she can receive a brochure that has pictures and persuasive language that shows and tells about all these elements.

When we are the customer, we want to feel special. Think the same way about treating your customers. Get a jump on your competition. When going to market, make it personal!

9. Understanding the Two Levels of the Power of Perception

<u>Level 1</u>: Our friends in the field of psychology tell us there are two primary elements that drive all human behavior. One is the desire to avoid pain. The other is the instinct to seek pleasure. Essentially, all successful marketing creates an expectation of one or the other (or both) happening through the purchase and use of a particular product or service.

Think about your own everyday experiences. We use things like sun tan lotion to avoid sunburn (pain) and purchase life insurance so those left behind aren't left in hardship. Going out to a nice dinner and using a particular personal hygiene item could both be described as pleasure-seeking experiences.

Pleasure and pain are very personal *perceptions*. And how individual consumers feel about your product will vary widely from person to person. But know this. It is the establishment of the *belief* that your product will avoid pain or help create pleasure that is the cornerstone of good marketing.

Level 2: As we've discussed, a key component of marketing success is your perceived level of credibility (PLC). This is a complex condition based on a wide variety of factors including: prior use of your company and products, the buying experience of a "friend," the appeal of your advertising, the reputation of your organization in the marketplace (good, bad, fair or not), the accuracy of your marketing message, the impression after contact with your salespeople and the ease in which you provide information.

One thing is for sure. If the internal abilities of your company differ from the external impression of the marketplace, you have a very large marketing challenge.

You may have the best people, newest equipment, best processes and highest quality product, but if you can't communicate that or worse, if your target audience *thinks* otherwise, sales will lag far behind what is possible.

Your goal must be to have the external impression equal very closely what your true internal abilities are. This will help to set the *expectations* of your prospective customers and give you the chance to meet and *exceed* them.

For the most part when you enter a McDonalds you know what to expect. The McDonalds *experience* is pretty much the same whether you are in New York City or Los Angeles, California. Two all-beef patties, special sauce, lettuce, cheese, pickles, onions on a sesame seed bun tastes the same in both places. And probably in Moscow, London and Paris too.

Like a good chiropractor fixing a bad back, get the market's impression in *alignment* with your positive abilities of value and watch the sales faucet flow.

10. Branding isn't just for cattle

While over time branding practices have sometimes been used for very inhumane purposes, I think most of us can associate with the herd of branded cattle being driven across the range in the old Western movies. The practice even existed in ancient Egypt as hieroglyphics from tomb walls clearly show the procedure taking place as early as 2000 B.C.

The use of brands in the American West allowed many ranchers to amass large fortunes through the application of their branding irons. Brands consisted of numerals, characters, letters, symbols, or a combination of these elements. Sometimes "rustlers" were able to change the brand slightly to one of their own to "appropriate" the value of the legitimate brand holder of the animals.

The branding of companies is of even greater importance to the marketer and today's organizations than the branded cattle were to the large ranch owner of the West. Yet there are many similarities. Certainly brands are a "hot" commodity and fortunes often rise and fall on the success or failure of the association of what the brand or brands of a particular company means to the prospective customers of that organization. A well-designed brand helps you establish your position in the marketplace – and can solidify your specialization in the minds of your prospects and customers.

Ultra successful brands can dominate a market segment to the point of renaming a product. Facial tissues are now "Kleenex." Many people carry a "Thermos" in their lunch boxes. And when you copy something many of us say we "Xerox" it. These brands actually absorbed the product category they were in.

Entrepreneurs know that they must be completely passionate about their brand. They live it, sleep it, eat it and dream about it all the time. It is that single-mindedness that drives them to communicate it to the world. This leads to recognition that leads to awareness that leads to great enterprises. Whether your brand is a product, a family of products, or the entire company, you must be passionate about what it represents to you and, hopefully, your customers.

Successful brands generally have at least some of these characteristics:

- <u>They are more than a logo</u>. While it is exceptionally vital to have the logo be displayed on all of your marketing collateral and advertising in a consistent, uniform manner, the name or symbol alone is not enough. The brand is representative of the *experience* and perception that prospects and customers have of a company. Buyers will associate strong feelings, positive or negative, with strong brands. Some people love Wal-Mart because it means ultimate selection and low prices in one place. Some people hate Wal-Mart because they think when one comes to town it puts small businesses out of business. Either way, the Wal-Mart brand evokes strong recognition and strong reactions.

- <u>But logos are important</u>. The Nike "swoosh" is an example of one that is instantly recognizable to most people, whether they use the equipment or not.

- <u>Brands convey personality</u>. The Merrill Lynch bull and the phrase "A breed apart" is instantly attractive to leaders who see themselves as ahead of the pack.

- <u>Can include taglines that convey the value proposition</u>. Federal Express' (FedEx) original "when it absolutely positively has to be there overnight" is about as clear as it gets as far as the mission for both the customer and the business.

Your brand won't convey the right idea for everyone, but executed properly, will convey your market position and value to the **right** customers. A great brand will help make you one rich "rancher."

11. Can you feel the Love?

Although marketing is supposed to be the job of marketing professionals, salespeople in all industries are still called upon to generate interest and find new customers. The old worn cliché that everyone is in sales (or is it marketing) remains true. As we'll see in the next chapter, finding 'em is still and always will be necessary for sales types as well. But marketing is always what happens before the 1st sales call.

So if this is true, where can we go, and with whom can we be enthusiastic enough, to create the excitement and make the connections we need to gain new customers? Instead of *grinding* your way through it, why not try to have fun all the while? Go and do what you like, meet some folks who have the same interests and watch the opportunities multiply.

In the end, the **right** customers will often be those you have the most in common with, no matter how you found them. People do business with people they relate to best. Few if any of us have the time to spend too much of it with people we really don't enjoy. While attempting to be a chameleon and morph yourself to be like, and enjoy, your customers' interests is possible, it is more practical, natural and fun to find folks who like what you like to do.

Several years ago we had a buyer at a large insurance company who gave us appointment after appointment but with no orders. We had done our marketing homework and had shown him how we had helped other people in his position at similar companies. Still no orders. After a couple of years of this we uncovered that he had just taken up the game of golf and like so many other "converts" had discovered a great passion for it. When we invited him to one of the many charity events we supported, he eagerly accepted. We had a wonderful time despite being in a golf cart for 6 ½ hours on a very rainy day. The *very next day* we had a purchase order faxed to us for over $25,000 dollars. Now while this may seem like bribery, after that we enjoyed a very long relationship and the company became one of our largest clients as we provided them with very beneficial products and services.

Think about the things you are excited about outside the office. This could include: charity, entertainment, sports, or any other kind of hobby. From a marketing perspective, find individuals who share your passion and connect with them.

Then watch as you grow new customers, have fun, and make friends all at the same time.

12. What are friends for?

Ask yourself. How many cold calls or mass mailing campaigns have worked out for you recently? Sure there are a few random successes but if you're honest with yourself, you will admit that these tactics had better not be the cornerstone of your marketing philosophy. Because of the skepticism of buyers today, and the pressure to increase sales in every industry is only increasing daily, the obstacles that customers have put up are harder to overcome than ever before. You get stuck in voice mail "jail," held up at the front desk, get asked to "send me information" and ignored by all manner of people. Gatekeepers are everywhere.

Of the more recent innovations in business development, the change in prospecting techniques is probably the most profound. While networking is nothing new, the sophistication of strategies is greater than ever. Networking is part of the process you go through in having your "friends" help you make more friends. There are three areas in which your friends can specifically help you achieve a greater level of success. Networking. Testimonials. Referrals.

1. <u>Networking</u>. Is there anything more ubiquitous than the local Chamber of Commerce event where sales professionals eagerly trade their business cards in hopes of selling to each other? While these can become an event where it is possible to become a wallflower equal to

a nervous high school student at a dance, you can learn to make these a resounding success. Several tips to make more friends include:

- Realize business cards are like gold. Make notes on the back of all cards and record brief notes of conversations, follow up dates and details of where you got it.
- Know when to stay in and when to get out of conversations. After meeting someone and understanding what they do, introduce them to others you've met who they can help.
- Have goals. Do you have someone you want to try to meet based on the event? Know what information you want to give away and get. Decide the number of people (quantity or quality) you need to meet.
- Have fun. Get out of your comfort zone. Smile. Display positive body language. Seek out strangers and go for it!
- Work your way in. Stand on the edge of a friendly group and be ready to jump into the conversation. Take your

opportunity to engage and entertain.

- Listen attentively and ask lots of who, what, where, when and why questions.
- Act like the host, not like the guest.
- Be ready with your 30-second commercial. Explain your value in terms of how you help solve problems for your customers.
- Focus on building connections instead of trying to close sales.

2. <u>Testimonials</u>.

One of the surest ways to increase your perceived level of credibility (PLC) is to have your good customers give testimonials to the benefit of working with you and your organization. This comes most often in the form of written letters. But don't ignore a video message as well. If you have a DVD or other similar type of video presentation about your business, this can be a powerful way to have your customers "speak" directly to your prospects.

Testimonials should not be a one-size-fits-all solution. Rather, tailor several different ones by asking your customers to speak to different situations that you and they experienced in the investigation process that led up to the decision to do business together. The true power of testimonials is that you don't have to do any persuading or selling; your customers do it for you. Some of the different types of endorsements you'll want to consider include:

- Taking a phone call: Have your current customer write a letter that you might include if you send out basic prospecting sales letters. This way when you make your follow up phone call you have included a credible 3rd party endorsement. Have your writer encourage the recipient that taking your phone call is a low-risk investment of time.

- To get an appointment: Many buyers, as you're probably well aware first hand, guard their appointment, giving time as if they were guarding the crown jewels. To break through this defense, have your testimonial writer mention that they too were hesitant to take the time to see you initially. But that, in the end, the meeting was well worth it and they have been a satisfied customer for some time.

- At proposal time: This can be even more helpful if you are in an industry where you can get three or four customers (probably non-competing) who are in the same "space" as your prospect. Chances are, they will have compared your offering against that of the same competition your prospect is. Showing your prospect that they all choose you will carry a lot of weight.

3. Referrals

There is perhaps no more powerful marketing tool than the personal endorsement from one individual to another about your product and service or even better, you! Despite what I like to think about the excellent marketing efforts for my own company, when we analyzed last year where our top 50 clients came from, **over 80%** came from a direct connection with a customer, friend or someone in our network of friends. There is no substitute for a "warm" introduction.

Many strategies abound about gaining a steady stream of referrals. Like many other points of view in this book, I don't believe there is one right answer for everyone. Instead, experiment and see what works for you. Some options include:

- Create an incentive program for current customers to offer names to you of potential users. But beware because there are two sides to this approach. Upside is that some folks will be happy to "grab" the goodies of whatever you offer for their help. Downside is that some people may be offended by the "sales" attitude (vs. customer care).

- Offer a similar incentive program to your own company's associates to provide "leads" to the marketing and/or sales department. This helps everyone feel that they can contribute to the overall revenue success.

- Ask the permission of current customers and networking partners to discuss referrals with them. Be sure to let them know you want to help them as well. Count on the power of reciprocation. Humans tend to be hard-wired to return in kind what they've been given. Give some to get some. Show me yours and I'll show you mine.

- When asking for referrals with current customers, be sure to discuss the benefits of what they've received and/or problems you've solved. This will strengthen their good feelings toward you (hopefully) and help focus their thoughts on who else might enjoy the same value you've brought them.

- Carry a "Hot List" or "Wish List." Create a list of the top two or three dozen prospects that you're hoping to start a conversation with this year. Show it to all the people with whom you come in contact. According to the rule of six degrees of separation, a high percentage of the people you show this list to will know at least a few people as your target prospects.

Marketing is good. Warm marketing amongst friends is better.

13. Be prepared to run the Marketing Marathon

History tells us a Greek man named Pheidippedes ran the original marathon. During a war between the Greeks and Persians in 490 B.C., he was requested to run back to Athens to announce the Greek victory. He ran all the way from his hometown of Marathon to Athens, a total of twenty-six miles. Upon delivering the good news, Pheidippedes dropped dead.

While our competitive business environment is challenging, hopefully none of us are "at war" with the competition. But our determination to stay the course and willingness to run a marathon may be the deciding factor in winning the race.

Many things will go against you in your effort to stay in communication with your target audience in order to win their attention, interest and business. Since the urgent can often supercede the important, sustained marketing efforts sometimes are a casualty of changing market conditions, and impatience over immediate sales results.

Marketing isn't a "quick hit" for immediate sales. Or a singular event meant to drive results forever. Marketing is more like working out. You don't do it once and stay strong forever. In the same way, to give your organization long-term sales "muscle," marketing needs to be an everyday, long-term commitment.

One of the first casualties of organizations (or industries) in a downturn is the marketing effort. One of the most common strategies is to cut prices and pull back on advertising. Both are the wrong answer, always, but certainly in times of adversity. Many studies have shown that in times of trouble, smart companies actually *increase* marketing activity. The result is invariably an increase in sales and market share because so many competitors are pulling back. Acquiring customers can be easier when others aren't even trying.

Over time, a marketing program that is committed to will: draw customers to you, generate a constant flow of new business leads, create a "presence" for your organization in the marketplace and focus the attention on the prospect instead of the product.

Though at times you'll be running at full speed, successful marketing is not so much a sprint as it is a marathon. Be prepared to go the distance.

14. Blow your own Horn

I've heard it said that you should blow your own horn or someone else will use it as a spittoon. Nowhere is this more true (and important) than in a competitive marketing and sales arena. Buyers ignore you, the competition is always trying to find ways to beat you and public perception is shaped by what you do, or don't do.

Of the more successful ways to shape favorable opinions of your company, product and service, the two favorites are clearly public relations and advertising. Put public relations efforts first and your advertising will be better recognized and better received.

Public Relations. Let your good deeds be noticed. Many organizations, for very altruistic reasons, make significant contributions to community causes and charitable concerns. And it is more than OK to let folks, some of whom are your prospects and customers, know of your assistance to these worthy endeavors. There is a two-for-one benefit to this. Raising public awareness can add to the help that a particular cause receives and can significantly enhance your reputation in the minds of the buying public.

The bank that makes a contribution to a local school program, the ice cream store that gives their sponsored little league team free ice cream after the game and the company that organizes a clothing drive for the Salvation Army are all examples of events that are "newsworthy."

Articles and pictures about your organization's good deeds in the press create awareness and dramatically improve your credibility. Go for quality over quantity, as it is the content of the stories that appear that is more important than the number of them.

Have a professional PR person create a media kit and work with you to discover publications and other media that your target audience will see and/or read. Just like targeting your markets, target your exposure outlets as well.

Some of the events you could try to "get attention" for include:

- Winning awards. Get involved in contests about your product and service and make sure to win. Articles written about "winners" carry great weight.
- Company Newsletters. Not yours but your customers. If you've done something of value for your clients ask for the story to be mentioned in the next edition of their newsletter. It will get you noticed by top management if you don't already have a relationship.
- New hires and promotions. Many local business journals and city newspapers carry brief "people on the move" sections where you can post changes within your own organization. It shows people things are happening at your company.
- Start a charitable foundation. People have an innate need to help. Tap into the collective power of your organization and get the entire workforce to rally around a specific concern. Sponsor events with maximum employee participation.
- Company milestones and economic contribution. Number of years in business gets people's

attention. Adding workers and helping employ more people are of particular interest

- Product launches, re-branding, and reengineering efforts. People like winners, and get interested in change. If you're introducing new products and services or establishing new missions, people will want to know what's happening.

Look for opportunities to enhance your reputation and improve your perception in the minds of the buying public. It will help oil doors that are hard to open.

<u>Advertising</u>: Advertising campaigns that win creative design awards are nice. Advertising that rings the cash register is better. Creative ideas won't work if they are deployed in the wrong media. Strategy and target markets will determine which ones are most likely to work for you and your company. But there are four absolutes that should be obeyed when you advertise in any manner.

1. <u>Use the right words</u>. Words that work are; you, your, how, new, save, discover, now, save, free, want, why, guarantee, proven, and money. They concentrate on the "what's in it for me" concept for the customer. Words to avoid include; I, we, us, our and me. Remember, it's not about you or what you think.

2. <u>State the difference</u>. All of the work of marketing is built upon showing and proving to your customer why they should buy from you and not your competitors. If you can't convey the differences, you either haven't done your homework well enough or you have nothing to say because you're not really different.

3. <u>Focus your message on your target audience</u>. If you've uncovered 200 out of 10,000 people whom you've concluded are your MLB prospects, spend your time and resources on the group of 200 and ignore the other 9800.

4. <u>Be specific</u>. Most adjectives such as *biggest* and *fastest* and unsubstantiated claims like superior and better solutions ultimately don't say anything. People ignore them. Try something more along the lines of "studies have proven that Acme's newest car gets 37% better gas mileage than all other brands, thereby saving you hundreds of dollars per year." Vagueness in advertising is the companion of apathy with the customer.

By combining directed public relations efforts with targeted advertising campaigns, you will blow sweet pleasing music out of your horn that will attract more people to your symphony.

15. Close the loop

Of all of the concerns that I have heard regarding marketing over the years (including at times within our own company) is something along the lines of: "Yeah, it looks great but how do I know it is working?" The problem is that too many marketing and/or advertising efforts can't show how and where the results are coming from. If they're coming at all.

We have used a formula for a while now that has generated superior results for our business and for our clients' businesses as well. It goes like this:

Strategize

Execute

Measure

Strategize. As we've alluded to, you want to target and cultivate those people and businesses that are Most Likely to Buy (MLB) your products and services. Very few organizations have the money or resources to try to reach everyone who *might* be a potential customer. So step one becomes a strategic exercise to understand who and how to target your own MLB target audience.

As we've also discussed, an almost limitless amount of information now exists that allows you to identify these individuals or groups. Don't cut corners here. Like the old cliché, you don't want to climb the mountain only to find out in the end you were on the wrong one. In the same way, a brilliantly creative, well-executed campaign will do you no good if aimed at the wrong target.

The main objective in finding your MLB prospects is to discover the **relevancy** of your product or service to them. You must consider yourself on a *need to know* basis about why your current customers buy from you so you can effectively communicate to potential buyers who are similar how they would benefit from your value proposition. This can be done through surveys, either on line, telephone or mailed, and on a larger scale, industry and/or consumer research including focus groups.

Execute. Many a general has gone down to defeat because of poor execution of the "battle plan." Armies (marketers and businesses) often get defeated not by the enemy (or competition) but too often it is by their own hand due to a lack of performance.

When coordinating your overall marketing effort, both strategic and tactical, you may find substantial benefits to working with organizations that merge both aspects "under one roof." Many of the breakdowns in execution can often be traced to poor communication. Like successful supply-chain management in logistical (warehousing and distribution) applications, successful communication management is often improved by shortening the links in the chain. Too many cooks in the kitchen often spoil the soup. Marketing firms who can handle the research, strategy, creative *and* production, assembly and distribution in-house can often offer a powerful ally in the streamlining of efforts and eventually a greater return on investment (ROI) for your marketing campaigns.

<u>Measure</u>. Like the old management saying goes, "You can't manage what you can't measure." In the same way, to become more sophisticated and have greater top-line impact on your organization, you must know the monetary return on your marketing investments.

Several advances in technology can now make this an easier task and help you close the loop in your marketing equation. With the cross-media campaigns described in the Make it Personal section, you can now drive both prospects and customers to a web site to update their own information and preferences. This allows you to know for certain who came to visit, what they looked at, how long they stayed and if they bought. By capturing all the particulars about every transaction, you have the ability to take your performance management measures right back to your strategy to tweak it to get better and better results.

Building this type of perpetual learning system into your data collection will allow you to conduct *memory-based* marketing campaigns, built on bi-directional communication between you and your audience.

By getting your total marketing effort aligned to continuously find and nurture your MLB prospects, your sales team can now come in and do their job. **Get 'Em.**

2
Get 'Em

"Salesmanship is limitless.
Our very living is selling.
We are all salespeople"

James Cash Penney

If your marketing efforts have been successful in attracting some potential buyers and there is more than just a simple call or mail-in-the-order process that follows, it is now time to send in the salespeople. Your marketing may have done some of the right things to generate interest and show your differences versus the competition in isolation, but now, your salespeople, either on the phone or in person, must "close the deal."

But unlike the stereotypical glad-handing salesperson of the past, professional salespeople today need a myriad of skills to pass the test of today's sophisticated buyers. Even if you have qualified inquirers, if you can't show value, if you don't bring something extra to the table, there will be no sale. With the multitude of choices for most products and services and the amount of information available, especially on the web, there is virtually no way to "fake it" in sales anymore.

Unless you are the proverbial "order taker," if there is some level of convincing or persuading people to buy from you, you must strive to develop the traits of winning salespeople. Bad salespeople try more tricks than a second-rate magician and are about as subtle as a piano falling out of a third floor window. Sales skills for success today include:

- <u>Empathy</u>: If you think it is about you and "hitting quota," you're guaranteed to miss the mark. Remember, it's not about you. As I've heard master sales trainer Zig Ziglar say many times, "You can have anything you want in life *if* you help enough other people get what they want first."
- <u>Listening</u>: You can't know what to sell if you don't know what they want. Like Stephen

Covey says in his book, *The Seven Habits of Highly Effective People*, "Seek first to understand..."

- <u>Organization</u>: "Winging" it doesn't work anymore. Customers won't waste time with you if you're not prepared. Be on time and on message.
- <u>Detail</u>: Pre- and post-sale planning, the ability to follow through on commitments and getting the specifics right the first time are critical to overall customer satisfaction.
- <u>Efficiency</u>: No wasted time in meetings, planning or execution.
- <u>Bottom-line oriented</u>. Top performers always show their customers the bottom line value to doing business with them and their company.
- <u>Insight</u>: Average salespeople can sell their product and service. Excellent salespeople know how that product impacts their customers' business. They differentiate themselves with creative ideas, adding value, and solving problems.

Simply put, people buy from people they trust, and buy what they need from people who understand what they want. Buyers buy emotionally. As sales trainer Jeffery Gittomer, author of the *Little Red Book of Selling*, is fond of saying, "it's actually much less about selling and much more about creating the conditions in which people want to buy."

1. Connect the Dots

We play a lot of games around our house and have many favorite activities. One of the favorites, as it was mine when I was a kid, is a book full of connect the dots pictures. I never fail to get excited as the lines get drawn from point to point until what was hidden on the page comes into sharp focus. Draw the lines wrong and the picture comes out wrong. Don't connect the dots and the picture remains a mystery. Following the instructions and directions, the process if you will, ensures a successful effort in the end.

In business disciplines like accounting and manufacturing there are well-defined processes that are followed very carefully to make the books balance and the products come out with consistent quality. Only in sales do we sometimes allow such a high degree of variability and then wonder why the results are inconsistent. Do you have a process you follow most of the time? Far easier to have a plan and allow exceptions than to live by exceptions and try occasionally to have a plan.

I heard a speaker say once that the only sustainable competitive advantage in the long run is the sales process. Products, companies and even entire industries will come and go. If you don't believe me ask the buggy whip manufactures and the blacksmiths how well they're doing. Other businesses have become successful by being flexible with change while retaining a structured way to continually generate sales results. You must have a repeatable process that puts things in the proper order to ensure long-term success.

When toilet training one of our children, we were amazed when he announced he was going to go to the bathroom by himself. Sneaking up to peek in the door we watched while he removed his pants, relieved himself, then flushed and washed his hands. Only after all that did he open the lid to the toilet, however. We praised him for the effort but putting things in a slightly different order would have generated a more successful result.

Make sure you know what appealed to people from your marketing effort. Analyze your successful and unsuccessful sales opportunities. What trends stand out? Are there common things you did in a common sequence that won the customer more often?

The picture only comes into focus when you connect the dots in the right order. Figure out which order your "dots" should get connected in and stick to it. You'll create many more beautiful pictures than by making up a random pattern every time.

2. Win friends to Influence People

Let's face it. You can't get along with everyone. We all have people with whom it just clicks and having a relationship is easy, like laying on the beach on a hot summer day. And there are those people that are a "grind," where every interaction is like sitting in a dentist's chair waiting for the oncoming drill. In sales, whether behind the counter, on the retail floor, or in the corner office, you are definitely going to meet "all kinds."

My marketing professor in college made a statement that has stuck with me until this very day. "Buyers buy because of the way they buy." Sure it's a way of saying folks buy for their own reasons but it is also because of their own *style*. It's much more likely (and necessary) to be the salesperson that must adapt rather than the customer. The lesson of the chameleon applies: change your appearance to suit your environment in order to survive.

If you think you can't, I read recently that even blind chameleons are able to alter themselves to ensure their safety. If they can do it, you can too. If you think it is too manipulative, remember this variation of the golden rule, you are doing onto them in the way they appreciate and respect. Although we talked earlier about the value of finding common-minded customers, it's not always going to be possible. You will need some strategies to earn the business of those with whom it is not quite as easy or smooth.

Dale Carnegie's classic *How to Win Friends and Influence People* is a good place to start. Timeless advice like: being appreciative, becoming interested in others, letting the other person talk more than you, and smiling – a lot, never goes out of style. But there are additional skills to learn that can help with your ability to sell more "kinds" of people.

- <u>Respect people's time</u>. In the hyper-competitive and downsized world we all live in, few of us usually have the time to waste with hyped up "product pitches," or to deal with salespeople who are not punctual for appointments. Learn, when necessary to be brief, be brilliant and be gone.

- Watch your body language and habits. I've had a bad back from time to time. The pain sometimes gets intense and if I sit in one position for more than a few minutes it can cause me to "fidget." I've been told by good customers (after being able to start a relationship despite this) that they did not think I was interested in them and was not focused. People will pick up on negative vibes--real or perceived.

- Generate Trust. Unless you are a bona fide expert, again, to begin with many folks are cautious of your motives. Don't say, "I think." Use the feel, felt, found model: "I understand why you *feel* that way, many of our current clients *felt* that way too, what they *found* in the end was...." Your clients have more credibility than you do at the time of the first sale. Or....

- Project Confidence. Many people want to deal with "winners." These customers want to know you have answers to their issues. Make recommendations and be decisive.

- Understand different personality and behavior types. Evaluations like the Myers-Briggs and the DISC profile can give you enormous insight into why other people think, act or buy in a certain way. And you might just learn something about yourself in the process.

If you're thinking it's a good idea to make more sales, learn how to make more "kinds" of friends.

3. Be like a Boy Scout

I discovered early on that I was not a "camp-out" kind of kid. Only lasted six weeks as a scout. And while all organizations get some criticism leveled at them at one time or another, you could do much worse than to emulate some of the ideals of the Boy Scouts.

The Salesperson's (Boy Scout) Oath

On my honor I will do my best to do my duty to my manager (God) and my company (country) and to follow company performance guidelines (the scout law). To help my customers (other people) at all times, to keep myself physically strong *(not a bad idea),* mentally awake *(pretty important)* and morally straight *(absolutely necessary).*

Some of the virtues of the Scout Law include:

1. Trustworthy: Prospects and customers demand nothing less.
2. Loyal: Your employer who gives you the paycheck deserves nothing less.

3. Helpful: To be successful in sales, customers will accept nothing less.

4. Friendly: Really now, what did being unfriendly ever solve?

5. Cheerful: You attract more with honey than you do with vinegar.

6. Kind: The world could use a little more of this, don't you think?

7. Brave: Salespeople have to overcome rejection of all kinds every day.

8. Clean: Neat appearance and polished shoes still count.

9. Courteous: Hard to get what you want if you offend people.

10. Thrifty: Your company will appreciate you making them money--your customer, saving it.

The Famous Scout Motto: **Be Prepared**.

Do you have your 30-second commercial ready when you get the chance to give it to a potential buyer? Do you have your business cards with you at all times? Do you understand that to be successful tomorrow means you need to be getting ready today? Do you go into every day and week with a well-defined list of priorities and things to do? Do you study trends that can affect your industry, product and career? Are you actively trying to learn new skills all the time to improve? Have you done your homework before each and every sales call to show the prospect or customer that you genuinely understand their business and goals?

Successful salespeople are like successful Scouts. Their compasses point north toward high ideals. And they are prepared for success, all the time. We may not get to walk old ladies safely across the street like a scout, but we can help prospects walk across the street into our business to become customers.

4. Break out your Trench Coat

People love mysteries--always have and I suspect (small pun intended) they always will. Whether in books, movies or on TV, crime solvers of every kind have been idolized for generations.

When I was a child I favored the Hardy Boys. Today my daughters still read Nancy Drew. My wife was a huge fan of Angela Lansbury's character of Jessica Fletcher in the TV series *Murder, She Wrote*. From the erudite Sherlock Holmes to the CSI genre of forensic thrillers prevalent today, a good mystery still excites the imagination and just begs to be solved.

There are many parallels between the super-star crime solvers and the super-star salesperson. Prospects and customers have "problems" that need to be solved. Sometimes they're aware of them, sometimes they're not. Either way, a good salesperson is like a good detective. Ask the right questions, solve the right problems, get the right conclusions, and earn the right customers.

Perhaps my all time favorite detective was Lt. Columbo, played by Peter Falk. In a twist from the traditional "who-done-it," where the audience had to guess along with the crime solver which suspect was actually the criminal, the *Columbo* series featured a unique reversal. All of the crimes were shown in advance so the audience knew the whole time who the guilty party was. The "mystery" became how Columbo was going to gather enough evidence to solve the crime.

With his rumpled overcoat, clenched cigar, tousled hair and confused demeanor, Lt Columbo (no first name ever given) did not look like anyone the criminals should worry about. But with his keen sense of perception, probing questions and persistent follow through, he never failed to catch the bad guys in the end.

How much of a detective are you? Do you ask more questions or talk more? Are you always looking for clues? If you are not trying to be manipulative (bad) and are genuinely trying to help the customer (good), you'll want to become the best detective you can be. Like Lt. Columbo's cases, all the "crimes" probably have been committed (although you may be able to prevent some future ones as well). And the client will usually know who-done-it. It is your job to get to the real answers and solve the mystery.

Look for clues everywhere. How the person acts or dresses. What does their office look like? Notice the other people in the company. Happy or sad? Competitor's boxes may be in the hallway or at the shipping dock. Have there been any articles about them in the paper recently. Can you get your hands on the annual report? Gather all the evidence you can to build your case that your product or service will solve the 'crime' of any problems they have.

Unlike the famous detectives who get to put people away, if you do your job properly you'll be springing the customer from jail with the solution you've uncovered for them.

5. No Gains without Pain

First appearing in Ben Franklin's *Poor Richard's Almanac*, the phrase has long been one of my favorites. Variations have been used for many marketing campaigns and it is firmly entrenched in the athletic and personal fitness world as a mantra of sacrifice for ultimate rewards.

As you move through your personal sales career, you'll undoubtedly experience plenty of pain due to learning curves, rejection, high expectations with occasional low performance and other challenges that the sales path presents. But the gains will surely come if you stick to it.

Equally if not more important however, is the concept of prospect pain. Remember, it is not about you. If that person is in your showroom or on your retail floor or if you find yourself at their office, you are there only because they want something. In some cases it is information about the marketplace and at other times they have genuine needs (pain) in some area and are investigating whether or not you have solutions (gain).

In sales it is virtually impossible to sell the prospect that is "all set." They will tell you they have no needs.

They have been with their current supplier for twenty years. They're just looking. Don't believe any of it. It may not be about you but if you're together it's not by accident. Remember, people don't have time to waste today either. If they're there, they're at least partially interested in something. If it's not just to get some free advice or information to share with their current supplier (to be avoided in most situations if possible), then they're there because they need to solve pain on some level.

Pain could be anything from the basic: "I need a new outfit to look good at the event" to "My shipping carrier is choking my supply-chain effectiveness." Where there is prospect pain – there can be sales gain.

There is another favorite kid's game that can be very effective here. Put on your detective hat (or trench coat) and relearn how to play twenty questions. Here are some that help uncover pain so you--and the prospect--can gain.

1. What about your current situation don't you like?
2. What about your current situation could be better?
3. Are your company goals for this on track?

4. Are your personal goals for this on track?
5. Does that bother you?
6. How do you know?
7. You've never had a problem with…?
8. You'll never have a problem with…?
9. How do you measure that?
10. So you're completely satisfied with…?
11. Other folks in your industry have issues with….Do you?
12. What one thing would you change if you could?
13. If I could give you a magic wand…..?
14. How much do you think that it costs?
15. What have you tried?
16. How did that work?
17. When was the last time you looked into that?
18. How much do you think it is costing the company?
19. Have you given up?
20. What were you hoping we could do for you?

Questions focus the attention where it belongs, on the customer. Good questions uncover the *pain* the customer had, is having, or may have in the future. Great questioners *gain* more credibility, more sales and more of the right customers.

6. Champagne and caviar or Beer and Pretzels

Our former credit manager used to have a favorite saying. "No ticket – No wash!" I'm not really sure where she got the saying from, but her message was crystal clear. No money – No service.

I learned this lesson the hard way (as most new people do) many years ago when I was a rookie sales rep. One day when I was out making the required cold calls I came across what I thought at the time was the greatest prospect ever invented. He loved my presentation, told me how great our offering sounded and assured me we were going to do a *lot* of business together. It was a medium-sized manufacturing company that had been around for many years. So I assumed that they had the money to pay for all the things we talked about that day (mistake #1).

Despite the concerns voiced by my manager that something did not feel right even after my impassioned speech telling him we had a live one (not listening to the experienced voice of reason – mistake #2), I plowed ahead with more calls and work on what the prospect said he wanted (throwing good time after bad – mistake #3).

After five or six visits and lots of time designing a program "just for him," the day came to bring in the proposal. I handed it over excitedly and waited for a response. "It looks great," he said. "I need a few days to think it over." That was the last time I ever saw him. When I finally connected about a month later on the phone after countless attempts, he explained that it was *a lot* more money than he wanted to spend.

This guy had the proverbial champagne taste and beer budget. Like at college when we would have preferred Heineken and ended up drinking generic "Beer" instead. It was a lesson I thankfully learned early and it took only one experience. Know how much money decision-makers are willing to spend to fix their problems.

And despite many buyers telling you they don't know, they do. No one goes out looking at BMWs when they can really only afford a Chevy. No one tours $1,000,000 homes when they can only afford a modest apartment. People who have the power to make decisions know how much, at least within a range, they have available or in a budget to solve a problem and buy products and services. It's your job to figure that out early in the process

It's OK to spend allotted time on people who have some budget, and much more time on people who have much more budget. It's your job to figure out who's buying the beer and who's popping the champagne.

7. Surprises are for Birthday Parties

My kids love surprises. I think most do. If you have kids and you've ever come home with something tucked behind your back, or gone on a "mystery" ride for the day to a secret destination, you know what I mean. Watch a child's face when they are given a surprise party. Or watch them rip through the pile of presents with wild abandon trying to learn what hidden treasures are inside. Their expression is usually one of sheer joy. I recall the day I brought the puppy home for Christmas one year, positioned strategically under my overcoat. The ensuing noise that followed caused me to check the house for structural damage the next day.

I've observed a funny thing, however: adults are typically not quite as fond of surprises as children are. Many that I know insist on knowing if something "surprising" is going to happen whether it is a night out, party or whatever. If I was going to play Jr. psychologist my guess is that many adults feel the need to be *in control* much of the time. Or maybe more accurately, most adults have a fear of being *out of control* most of the time.

In the buyer/seller relationship, both parties want control. Buyers don't want to feel they got taken advantage of. And sellers don't want the relationship or sale to be just about providing the lowest bid. A paradox if there ever was one.

A smart salesperson knows that most prospects and customers don't want surprises during the buying process (unless they are unexpectedly pleasant or favorable to their position). A good salesperson is able to remain (mostly) in control of the process while helping the buyer feel that they are as well. Try to get as much upfront clarity with all of the "next steps" in the investigation process as possible.

- If sending a sales letter, state clearly your objectives and reasons for connecting with the individual(s). Cleverness in a letter usually doesn't impress but annoys.
- When following up on a sales letter say, "I'll follow up with a phone call on Tuesday the 5th between 9:00 and 9:15 AM." Then do it. It

builds credibility that you are a person of your word and punctual.

- When talking on the phone for the first time, again state very clearly the purpose of your call. Ask if you've gotten the person at a good time and let them know how much time you're asking for both for the call and visit if you can get one.

- Send a note or email confirming the meeting time and place and, if appropriate, the agenda you have agreed on.

- Be on time (which means 5-15 minutes early) for the appointment. This gives you time to go over any notes at the last minute and look for additional clues to bring up in conversation.

- Stick to your agenda and time frame. Deviate only if the other person has shown interest or given permission.

- Agree upon very clear next steps, if any, that will take place in further discussions.

- Send a copy of what was discussed, and agreed upon, *in writing*, by mail or email to avoid any misunderstandings.

Surprises are great for kids. They are not usually welcomed by adults, and definitely have no place in a successful sales process. Save the hats and noisemakers for the celebration after you've earned the business.

8. Know when to Fold 'Em

The goal of Finding 'Em, Getting 'Em and Keeping 'Em is all about creating a successful and repetitive process that earns you more business. But the right business. And the right customers. It does you, and ultimately the prospect, no good to start up the wrong relationship for the wrong reasons.

While not a perfect science, there are clues that will lead you to put some opportunities on hold for some period of time, or forever.

- Without a good reason, the prospect does not show up for an appointment that has been scheduled and confirmed. If they seem to have a legitimate reason, but don't show up twice, you might want to confirm that they really want to meet..
- The prospect keeps everything very "close to the vest" and does not share enough information to allow you to know how to help.
- If you hear "static on the street" about payment problems with other suppliers.
- You have been asked for and delivered three or more quotes without winning any of the business.

- You are asked for lots of information without any guarantee of future business.
- Every negotiation ends up as a win-lose in the customers' favor.
- The buyer comes up with last minute requests after the terms of a deal have been agreed upon.
- The prospect will not commit to anything concrete and next steps remain very vague.
- The communication goes "radio-silent" on the prospect's end after you've shared information, quotes or a proposal.
- There is a philosophy difference (i.e. you sell value and partnerships and the prospect is looking for three "bids" on every project).
- Depending on the circumstances, the prospect is not willing to share their budget with you.
- The customer's buying cycle is too long or too complicated.
- You can't see a way to make an acceptable profit on a particular customer.

Develop an attitude of abundance. Know that there are enough opportunities out there that are a good fit. You don't have to squeeze yourself into relationships and deals that are two sizes too small. Look for the warning signs. If you are not sure, remember the old proverb, "Fool me once, shame on you, fool me twice shame on me."

Being persistent and staying with 'em for a while is important. But none of us will make every sale and the better you can get at deciding which ones to chase and which ones to leave will go a long way toward determining your success.

Like Kenny Rogers' famous lyric said, "You got to know when to hold 'em and know when to fold 'em."

9. It's Showtime!

For baseball fans in New England there is always a gnawing sense of anticipation when getting ready for the start of a new season. Despite the long-awaited 2004 World Series victory of the Boston Red Sox, the region still turns its collective consciousness toward the thrill of a new chase beginning on opening day. After all the practice, and all the preliminary preparations involved with spring training, the first game arrives. When it really counts. Play Ball!

In the sales process, game day is sharing the proposal or making the presentation. Just like the ballplayers who spend countless hours and repetitive drills getting ready for the action that counts, a top sales performer will spend significant time and focused effort in preparing for the moment of truth, the presentation.

In baseball you must throw it, hit it and catch it. In sales you must create a proposal that includes a strong executive summary and/or generate an engaging presentation.

<u>Executive Summary</u>. The most read, and therefore potentially the most influential part of your proposal, is the executive summary. Create a sense of value here and your odds of winning the big game go up. Consider these four elements for maximum impact.

1. Explain the problem, plan, goal or opportunity. Show that you have a firm grasp on the business situation of the prospect.
2. Define the desired and expected outcome. Communicate the potential-positive-impact or the avoided-negative-impact on the customer's business.
3. Share the solution. Be very specific as to the suggestions and processes you are recommending and how it solves the issues in number one.
4. Make a call to action. There are two camps regarding asking for the order. If you're in the camp that thinks it is the right thing to do, here is the place.

<u>Sales Proposals</u>. Ones that don't work:

- Are "boiler-plate" and do little to customize from prospect to prospect
- Are written from the seller's point of view instead of the buyer's
- Don't include a strong executive summary
- Does nothing to highlight your differences versus the competition

With the increasing sophistication of buyers and the amount of information available to compare options, a winning proposal is only increasing in importance. Ones that work best:

- Help continue to sell even when you're not there.
- Are thorough and detailed in regard to answering all the prospect's questions or concerns.
- Reaches decision-makers that the salesperson can't.
- Convey a message that is consistent with your brand and image.

<u>Presentations</u>. Maybe a better analogy than opening day would be the Super Bowl. There's usually only one chance to win the big game. Presentations that sell have these qualities.

- Despite my use of them here, limit the bullets and go for something more attention-getting. Don't put your best points by bullets on a power point slide. It will make attendees beg for a "seventh-inning stretch" due to boredom. Instead, use some drama. Try to come up with a creative example of what using your product would mean. Stand out from the crowd to be remembered.

- Ditch the canned "pitch." Do your homework and know all the players who are going to be in the room and what each one thinks is important. Tailor your presentation to meet the needs of all who will be involved.

- Stay on message. In political speak, candidates try to stick with their talking points. Trying to ad lib too much can lead you down paths that have no relevancy to the prospect. If you've done the research and know what they're looking for – go with the plan you came with.

- Make a personal connection. While you're there to "perform," don't forget it is real people who are going to make the ultimate decision. No connection – no sale.

Ballplayers and sales professionals play "make pretend" in practice hundreds of times to make sure on game day they are ready to perform – and win!

10. Become a great communicator

The late former President Ronald Reagan was often referred to as "The Great Communicator". He earned this title by being able to resonate with the passions of the American people. President Reagan was able to work with the biggest of ideas, mold them to suit his philosophy and goals but keep them simple and understandable to most people. He could generate a call to action and build trust among his constituency. While it is unlikely we will ever command the world stage for our audience, we can learn some basic sales communication strategies to engender interest, trust and action.

Critical Points of Contact (CPC). During the sales process (on the selling side) or the investigation process (on the buying side) there can be many firsts, or opportunities to build rapport and demonstrate interest. While more communication is not always better communication, showing constant appreciation and commitment is not likely to be a bad thing.

1. The sales letter: As we've already mentioned, avoid the vague or clever. Be clear with what your value proposition is and what you're asking for (i.e. an appointment). Mention a

specific follow-up time or action, then be sure to follow through.

2. After the first telephone contact: Send an email or even better, a personal note (in an envelope with a stamp), with a brief message that you enjoyed the conversation, whether there is going to be a follow up meeting or not.

3. After the first appointment: Again, acknowledge your appreciation for the meeting and confirm all next steps, if any. Repeat the process for any new people you meet during the process.

4. After the first order: Make sure the new customer knows that you sincerely appreciate the new relationship. Get senior managers or owners to send a note, maybe along with a small gift as well, if appropriate.

Obviously, in a multi-step process or a sales cycle that lasts weeks or months, many times these steps could be repeated with some variation.

<u>Become someone with whom people like to speak</u>. While there are plenty of resources to learn about open and closed probes and "static" in the communication channel, I prefer a very simple model to ensure more authentic conversation. I've heard this model mentioned in several places, first by Dr. Ken

Blanchard, author of *The One Minute Manager*. It's called the **E.A.R**. model

Explore: Good salespeople don't assume too much and don't practice mind reading, they ask questions. Load your interviews with Who, What, Why, How, When and Where questions.

Acknowledge: This is your chance to demonstrate empathy. "Gee, I can see how you feel that way based on….".

Respond: Convey your understanding when you get the gist of what the person is telling you. "So what you're saying is that…." This helps prove to people you are listening to what they've said and you get what is important.

Great salespeople are great communicators. They build credibility and interest through their actions. And they build customers through their listening and concern for others.

11. Make tomorrow's sale Today

In the Michael J. Fox movie, *Back to the Future,* the character of Marty McFly goes back in time to ensure that his future will turn out right. Countless Star Trek episodes and Sci-Fi thrillers have used the same theme.

In sales, sometimes you need to go into the future to make today's sale. An aware retail salesperson knows how to suggest a tie to go along with a shirt or shoes to go along with a suit. He or she can project a picture of the future without the proper attire to secure the current sale and get an extra one as well.

Good business-to-business salespeople rarely have only one product or service to sell. They also know that if the first product has some value to the buyer, others may as well. And top salespeople are so tuned in to their prospects or customers' business they are able to make valuable suggestions for additional services. If you can help the buyer see how the whole picture ties together for their benefit, you raise the odds of getting the first sale as well.

A printing company should ask the customer if the printing project needs to be mailed. A warehousing company might ask if the stored items could be packaged in a certain way to improve efficiency. A flooring company who installs carpet in the living room can ask if the homeowner would like the hardwoods in the dining room re-finished. No product or service is an orphan. They are always related in one way or another to something else.

Help the customer see the big picture by showing how one thing complements another. In selling, "it's the hip bone is connected to the..." kind of thinking. By linking one sale to another and showing the customer the added value, you make today's sale, and maybe tomorrow's as well.

12. Fire the Sales Prevention Department

Inside many organizations there is a secret department. It has no budget. It has no titles. It is not listed on the organization chart. Yet it has a powerful impact on results. And the results are always negative. The sales prevention department is a stealthy organization that steals potential revenue by getting in the way of sales productivity.

There are several kinds of people and circumstances that are part of this department.

- <u>The internal naysayer</u>: Salespeople have enough to overcome with the daily rejection from prospects and the battles with the competition. Don't allow negative co-workers to drag down the enthusiasm of your salespeople.

- Inflexibility and stubbornness: "We've always done it this way" has been the death knell of many a business.

- Paperwork: Dotting the i's and crossing the t's is vitally important. But when it gets in the way of your salespeople making sales, find another way to get it done. When salespeople are doing paperwork, they're not selling.

- Insufficient tools: In this day and age, laptops, cell phones and customer relationship management (CRM) systems are not a luxury but a necessity.

- Lack of investment in training: There are very few "born" salespeople or customer service representatives. Most need to be cultivated through specific and focused training in selling skills, product and industry knowledge, and other trends that affect your business and their career.

- Effective sales literature and marketing collateral: Most buyers want as much information about your company as possible before making commitments. If you have out-dated or incongruent sales material or websites, you run the risk of not being considered at all.

- <u>Making it easy for the customer to buy</u>: In our instant gratification society, convenience is king. If you don't have easy ways for people to pay for your services (i.e. credit card or checking withdrawal plans) then you risk customers signing up with businesses who can.
- <u>Company policy</u>: While having procedures and policies is a good and necessary thing, don't let them get in the way of generating revenue and building relationships.
- <u>Company politics</u>: Never let large egos, jealous attitudes or turf wars get in the way of making sales.
- <u>Lack of knowledge sharing</u>: It is vital that successful case studies and company capabilities are communicated regularly to take full advantage of all possibilities.

Like an enjoyable symphony, a business works best when everyone is on "the same sheet of music." John Wooden, the famous UCLA basketball coach once said, "Don't let what you can't do stop you from doing what you can do." You may not have full control of the competition, the economy, technology and many other factors. But you can banish internal barriers to sales productivity. Start today by identifying and removing all the things in your control that are preventing more sales from happening.

13. Selling by the numbers

Quality, price and service: These are the traditional big three issues for most prospects and customers. There was a time when a product or service produced or provided at a competitive price, with acceptable performance and delivered on time, was all you needed. Not anymore.

Sophisticated buyers today who are armed with an almost endless supply of information and options now demand more. Quality, price and service might get you in the game, but they will not win it. Customers need to have *proof* of how you impact their business. The best way to do this is to show how you impact the customer's top line, their bottom line, or improve their efficiency. Take the fuzzy out of fuzzy math.

Top line: How can you improve the revenue line for your clients? Let's say you're an advertising sales representative for a local paper. Can you show the local pizza parlor how running ads in your paper has increased sales for other similar establishments? Maybe you ran a coupon with the ad that customers redeemed. Show in exact dollars and cents the increased revenue for following your program.

Bottom line: How can you show your customers you can save them money? The plumbing and heating company which sells gas furnaces must come up with a dollar and cents argument why switching from the oil furnace will save money (over time) even with the up front investment.

Increased efficiency: How do you convince the manufacturing company you can improve output? Show them irrefutable evidence that by using your equipment or people, they can increase production without increasing costs.

Get used to report card relationships: Tell your customers you want to be graded. Be proactive in establishing custom service level agreements. Insist (politely, of course) on informal 90-day reviews to track progress on goals and monitor creative suggestions you have provided. Successful long-term relationships will be based on moving the customer's "dial" in a positive direction. Share with the prospect or customer the monetary consequences of using or not using your product or service.

Return on investment (ROI) is not just for the stock market anymore. It is an absolute necessity for earning and keeping customers for both the short and long term. You are going to have to be able to **prove** to the customer that $1 invested with you is more beneficial to them than the same $1 with your competitor.

Show 'Em the Money!

14. Are we having fun yet?

Selling has often gotten a very bad, and very unfair, reputation over time. From the earliest "snake oil" salesman through plaid-suited door-to-door salespeople and two-tone-shoe car salesman, the profession has not always been held in the highest esteem. And while there certainly have been individuals who have manipulated prospects and taken advantage of customers solely for their own advantage, the vast majority of sales professionals are well-intentioned and provide excellent service and value to their clients.

Don't ever let others' opinions or the "pressures" of the job stop you from enjoying it. Selling is an honorable and important profession that you should enjoy *more* than most people enjoy other jobs. Whether telephone, retail, wholesale, business-to-business, business-to-consumer or any other kind of position, *selling should be fun,* or you should probably find something else to do.

Here are five reasons to have fun selling:

1. <u>You are an equal partner with the customer</u>. One of my pet peeves as a sales manager was when a rep said "Thank you for seeing me" or "Thanks for your time." Not that I did not want them to be appreciative. But "I'm glad we could get together" is much less *subservient* and positions you on the same level as the buyer. Selling and buying should be an *even* exchange of value. Without the customer – no sale. Without you – no value to the customer.

2. <u>Effort usually turns into results</u>. Hustle is an attitude. More hustle, more opportunities. In many cases sales is still a numbers game. More hustle, more opportunities. More opportunities, more results.

3. <u>Results usually generate rewards</u>. Sales is the best profession to be in if you want rewards that are equal to the results you can generate, for your customers, your company and you.

4. <u>You can genuinely help people</u>. If you possess a need to serve, a sales career offers a wonderful opportunity to accomplish your goals. A successful salesperson helps create value, makes their customer, their customers' organization, and their company more successful.

Great salespeople create jobs, keep people employed, and create wealth and prosperity for all with whom they come in contact.

5. <u>All of life is selling</u>. Sales skills are not just for buying and selling. The better selling skills you develop for your job, the more you can contribute and accomplish in every area of your life.

Selling should be fun and rewarding. If it's not, try to find ways to make it fun, or find something else to do.

15. Say thank you – and mean it!

Finally. While some sales may be a one-time close, most are much more complicated, especially in business-to-business sales. To secure the deal it may have taken several or many meetings over a few weeks or months, or more. Now is the time to finally celebrate and say thanks.

One of the surest ways to get the customer relationship started poorly is to take for granted the decision that was just made to hand you the business. Sales, as in life, requires an attitude of gratitude. How you say thank you will depend on the size and scope of the sale and the "rules" of the new customer's organization about such things in some cases. In the end, again as in life, it is usually the thought that counts the most.

The example of this I remember the most was some time ago when my wife and I first got married. At that time of your life you are (or at least we were) very busy consumers. We bought a new house and a new car and new furniture all in the span of two weeks leading up to the wedding. But the experiences could not have been more different.

First, the mortgage company, who made a sale for **hundreds of thousands** of dollars, who made it ridiculously complicated for us at the last minute (more on that in the next chapter), who never even bothered to send a meager house warming gift, who never sent a survey to see how the experience was, who never earned our business again despite numerous refinancings and additional home purchases.

Second, there was the car dealer, who made a sale for **tens of thousands** of dollars, who sent a "stock" letter of thanks from the general manager, who was hard to reach when we had some questions about the new car, who didn't return calls when we had problems with the new car, who never earned our business again despite buying over a dozen cars since then.

And third, the furniture store, who made a sale for a **few hundred** dollars, who sent a note of thanks signed by the sales rep (with a personalized PS regarding some of the things we talked about), who placed a follow-up call to see if we were satisfied with our purchase, who has received almost all of our furniture purchases over the last twenty years.

In most cases it probably doesn't matter what you do, just that you do something. It could be a small gift, a phone call from a manager or a personal letter from the president.

Don't be too quick to move on to the next sale. Make sure you anchor in the customer you just sold first. Say thank you – and mean it. After Getting 'Em, making sure the transition is smooth and the business is sincerely appreciated is the most important step to **Keeping 'Em**.

3
Keep 'Em

"There is only one boss.
The customer and he can fire everybody
in the company from the chairman on down,
simply by spending his money somewhere else"

Sam Walton

Now comes the hard part. Anyone can get a customer to buy the first time. It's the ultra-successful organizations that get people coming back over and over again. Customer service is not an attitude that can be turned on or off on a whim. It is an all-pervasive philosophy that permeates every layer of successful organizations. In today's hyper-competitive marketplace, buyers demand and accept nothing less. They need to "feel the love" on a regular basis as the saying goes.

And customer service is not just for the people with that title on their business card; it is for everyone in the organization, whether they come into contact with the customer directly or not. Customer service is *everything* that the customer sees, feels, touches, hears, smells and **experiences** throughout the buying process. From the person on the end of the phone to the appearance of the showroom, to the cleanliness of the bathroom, it all goes into the impression of value you create for the prospect or customer.

There are really only three possible outcomes for a business transaction from the customer's point of view. You could fall below expectations. You could meet expectations. Or you can exceed expectations, only one of which gives you the chance to lock-in future repeat business. The Law of Reciprocation states that when someone does you a favor you do one back. Customers who feel that they got more value than they deserve will feel inclined to reciprocate – with more orders!

Simply put, customer service is the things you do, or don't do, that will increase the likelihood of a customer buying again. And again. Expressed in a formula or equation it might look like this:

$$A\$V + 2E = LC$$

(Actual dollar value + exceeding expectations in performance, quality and service = loyal customers).

The actual dollar value is how much you have saved, how much you have earned, or how much more efficient you have made your customer. By exceeding expectations you build perceived value that is greater than the investment. And a loyal customer is one that both does not take their business elsewhere, and brings their friends to you as well.

1. What does good service look like?

We have probably all experienced it in one way or another. We bring the item we just purchased home from the store. We plug it in, turn it on or put it on and it doesn't work the way we *expected* it to. We then read the manual but can't find any useful information. We call the 800 number and must painstakingly navigate the automated phone system, only to be placed on hold. We end up frustrated and confused and unhappy with the purchase and the company who sold us the item.

The question is, how much of this could have been avoided if the company or salesperson had explained how the product *should* work. In some cases, customer expectations are built on advertising, and in many cases personal perception. It's our job to explain, in detail, how something works and what performance the customer is reasonably able to expect from the product or service. Good service begins with setting up customer expectations so that they are not disappointed when things go the way they should, but rather, are happy to see they did.

When we buy our kids a toy at the local dollar store and later in the day it falls apart we are not surprised. We expected it. It performed about a dollar's worth of value. When the $100 toy that comes home from Toys R Us takes us three hours to put together and falls apart within three minutes of being played with, we are not quite in the same good mood. The expectation we probably had was that the ease and performance would be far greater. But if it clearly said on the box: assembly time three hours, we would have known what to expect (or not bought it in the first place).

Expectations are different from industry to industry and product category to product category. We don't expect a pizza parlor to have the same quality of food or service (experience) as a fancy Italian restaurant. An airplane trip across country is far different in first class than it is in coach, and we're willing to pay for that. But beware the competitor who changes the rules of the game.

Southwest Airlines turned the airline industry on its head with low fares, friendly service and being "on-time." Domino's Pizza revolutionized the take out meal world with a guarantee of having a meal at your door in thirty minutes. Federal Express changed the package delivery universe with the ability to get it there overnight. Good service begins with telling customers what to expect and working like crazy to make sure it happens. But sometimes good service is also keeping up with the competition or risk being left in their wake.

When I was a 10-year-old in the dentists' chair getting my fillings, it was a terrifying experience. A man would come in, say open up, strap five pounds of equipment to my face, take out a drill and have at it. There were no expectations built about what was going to happen or why. In my head I was sure it was going to be an extremely unpleasant experience and my fears were always realized.

Fast-forward thirty years to the very few times my kids have had to have a filling. Now the dentist comes in, and mentions that there will be a slight "pinch" when they get a shot of Novocain that will make their mouth numb. Then he'll explain what the appliances that go over your mouth are for. And he'll say how fun it is to wear sunglasses inside. And that the drilling will only take five minutes and you won't feel it. The kids shrug, say OK, and get it done with no fuss and no fear.

Kids walk out smiling, not that it's over, but that it was no big deal.

In its own way that is an example of excellent customer service. The dentist (seller) took the time to explain to the patient (buyer) what was going to happen, what to expect before, during and after the procedure, and that it would be OK in the end. And when expectations are met, people walk out happy.

2. Treat 'Em this way

What does the "average" customer look like anyway? I'm not sure I've ever seen one. Henry Ford's famous statement, "they can have it in any color as long as it's black" would not play very well today, I think. Choice has become the dominant influence in the marketplace. Where once customers were "shoehorned" into what was available, now suppliers must create what customers desire or lose out to those who do. In an era in which variety knows almost no limits, you must have or develop the ability to service customers *individually* according to their wishes and expectations.

The explosion of choice during the last twenty-five years of the 20th century was truly astonishing. As reported in the book, *Differentiate or Die* by Jack Trout and Steve Rivkin, consider that there was:

- A 100% increase in the number of vehicle models
- A 300% increase in the number of McDonalds food choices
- A 400% increase in SUV models
- A 400% increase in the number of bottled water options
- A 500% increase in the number of dental flosses
- A 500% increase in the number of TV screen sizes
- A 700% increase in Frito-Lay chip varieties
- An 800% increase in the number of Colgate toothpastes
- A 900% increase in Pop-Tart flavors

- An increase from 5 to 285 of running shoe options
- From none to almost 5,000,000 web sites to choose from

With the ability today to divide the population into well-defined niche markets based on demographics, past buying trends and other data-related factors, the onus is on creative suppliers of products and services to anticipate needs and wants to serve each market segment in specific ways. Who would have ever dreamed that you could design an entire car on demand, online and have it delivered to you with all the specifications and options you wanted in just a couple of weeks?

What Burger King realized many years ago has become a reality for many industries today. And the trend of customization will only intensify for most products and services in the future. Customers are demanding individual treatment, and the companies who win will say, "Have it your way"!

3. Leave the multi-tasking to the moms

My wife is an amazing woman. I think most moms are. The very few times when she has been sick and

I've done the house and kid thing, it has not been pretty. She is able to cook a meal, sooth a crying child, feed a baby, help with homework, be on the phone arranging a classroom party and work on her laptop all at the same time.

In our everything-must-get-done-all-at-once culture, not balancing multiple priorities and cramming five pounds into the proverbial three pound bag is seen as a sign of weakness. The problem is that this is a very poor way to execute customer service in just about every possible situation. It could be titled 'how to annoy a customer and make them *not* feel special.'

In one of my favorite department stores I've noticed that the sales associates on the floor helping customers are also handling incoming phone calls. The problem is--which one do you take care of first? It certainly can't be both at the same time. If you put the customer on hold for too long, they'll hang up and who could blame them. If you try to help the person on the phone, the customer in the store might walk out (and I have – hope they don't blame me).

There was a sandwich restaurant near our office we used to visit (since closed – coincidence?) about once a week. The people behind the counter were trained, for perceived productivity reasons one can only assume, to take the orders of 4-5 people at one time and then verbally bring the requests back to the person who would then make the sandwich. Problem was, by actual count, nine out of ten times they had to come back and ask again what it was that someone wanted. And also by actual count, the order came back wrong four out of five times despite being asked twice what a given customer wanted. In the end, all the annoyed customers found somewhere else to eat.

In the long running comedy series MASH, the character of Dr. Charles Emerson Winchester, played by the actor David Ogden Stiers, made a comment I have remembered for a long time and it applies here. He said, "I do one thing at a time, I do it very well, and then I move on." If you want to make your customers feel special and keep them coming back, try it.

4. How are we doing?

The Winter Olympics just recently concluded. I'm not a fan of all the sports. There are too many events that have "style" points. Very subjective. Who you like or do not like is based on personal opinion. Give me the athletes who jump the highest, throw the farthest or move the fastest. While watching the speed skaters race around the track, their coaches could be seen yelling encouragement as well as informing each skater how fast they were going. They needed to know how they were doing in relation to their goal of how fast each lap should be skated. The skaters needed to plan ahead of time the desired time result if they were to be medal contenders. Feedback is the breakfast of champions.

Customer service champions blend both of these philosophies together to achieve superior results. They are able to pull off "style" points that are unique to each customer while achieving concrete measurements of excellent performance. They are very specific as to the desired results and stay on track the whole way to ensure they know how they are doing. Individuals and organizations that excel in customer service master several different ways to get the feedback they must have to be successful over time.

- <u>They ask</u>. Train your sales people and customer service people to ask both open ("How are we doing?") and closed ended (Did you enjoy the dessert?") questions of your customers often.
- <u>Response cards</u>. Either at the counter, on the table, in the package or handed out, these

tools create an easy way for the customer to share their experiences.

- <u>Surveys</u>. Either in the mail, on line or on the phone, periodic semi-formal inquiries show to your customers that when you say you value their opinions it is more than lip service.

- <u>Focus Groups</u>. When the need is for highly detailed information, properly conducted, these events can give you invaluable feedback both pro and con.

- <u>Customer Advisory Panels</u>. Want to keep your best customers involved at a deeper level? Sponsor regularly scheduled meetings with a diverse group of your better customers. Having a voice in your direction helps ensure you understand what your customers truly need and it increases their loyalty.

Successful organizations focus deeply on understanding what their customers need from them, now and in the future. Average businesses are vendors, bidders, or suppliers for their customers. Great businesses are partners and strategic resources for their customers. The better you are able to get to know your customers, the better you can serve them. The better that your customers can get to know you, the more they will buy.

Knowing how you're doing in the eyes of your customers is the only way to climb the value ladder – and keep 'em for the long run.

5. Know where your Bread is Buttered.

Recently I walked into an establishment where four of my children regularly attend classes. Having so many involved at one time, we've obviously gotten to know many of the people there and I engaged in some pleasant conversation. When it came time to depart and hand over the check the lady behind the desk said to me, "Thanks for helping to keep the lights on," to which I replied, "I help keep the lights on at a lot of places."

Now I know most of you probably don't have eight kids. And your local grocery store manager probably does not jump up and down with glee for you like mine does when he sees me approaching. But the fact of the matter is we all help "keep the lights on" everywhere we buy things, just as our customers do for us. And the heat for the buildings. And the electricity for the machines. The reality is, everything they get comes from us and everything we get comes from them. What comes around goes around. That's why everyone is (or should understand they are) involved in customer service.

While IPOs or investors might generate some money for a business at its inception or for a special event, in the long run it's the day-to-day customers who pay the bills. And the paychecks. Want more money? More employees? Expansion? Acquisitions? Get and keep more customers.

While you want to treat all customers special, make sure you know who the "A" customers are. The 80/20 rule will probably show you that 80% of revenues come from 20% of your customers. Treat 'em all special if you can, just treat this group *extra* special.

A word of caution about making hasty judgments, however. Be sure you know the relationship that each of your customers have with each other. If some are business units of a larger customer, or have been a steady source of referrals to you, make sure they don't get second best treatment.

At the end of the day, it's our customers who have put the butter on our bread.

6. Reach out and touch Someone.

We've all seen the commercial. The elderly woman sits in front of her window staring blankly while rocking away in her rocking chair. A heavy sigh comes out because no one *cares* about her. The next moment the phone rings. It is a loved one calling "just because" to have a conversation. Cut to the end of the commercial seeing the same woman staring out the same window but now with a contented smile on her face. Someone cares after all.

While your customers are not likely sitting waiting for you to call, you can assume that your competitors are calling them, frequently. How well are you showing customers that you care – on a regular basis? Although very few (if any) of us have time for pointless communication, we all like to be appreciated and informed about important matters. Make sure your retention efforts are full of multi-channel communication (mail, email, web, fax, phone, visits) that convey you appreciate the business, are a resource by keeping customers informed, and are making offers of additional services.

Consider the following potential "touch points" as part of your retention program:

- Put stuffers in your statements or invoices about additional products or services. Feature a new one each month.

- Create an automatic email from the appropriate manager acknowledging if there has been a quality or service issue. Assure the customer the matter is important, being looked into and will be resolved very quickly.

- Use your database to send "random" thank you notes from each salesperson to each contact at each customer once per year. Just because.

- Publish a newsletter at least twice per year to inform customers about "newsworthy" events or changes in your organization that might have a positive impact on them.

- Contract with a media service that lets you know about events that happen among your customers (product launches, promotions etc.). Send notes of congratulation.

- Have the President or VP of sales send a Thanksgiving letter to "thank" customers for their business during the year, extend holiday wishes and discuss anything that might impact the coming year.

- Have executives at your business (VP Operations, VP Finance etc.) contact their peers at your customers' business. Sometimes when people "speak the same language" additional opportunities can be created because they don't feel they are being sold by a salesperson.

- Send your current marketing materials, especially if you've recently changed something or added something. Don't leave it up to your salespeople to do all the education.

- Send promotional products to reinforce your name/brand recognition or again, announce new products, services, or a new web site.

- Send special offers that apply only to customers. Give them the opportunity to get in on things before anyone else.

- If you don't know, find out what interests your customers have outside the business. Take them to a play, ball game or a wine tasting. Building deeper relationships and having fun at the same time is still OK.

Show your customers that you care and strive to provide value in your communication. A successful retention program helps promote happy, loyal customers. You want that little old lady expecting your call, and looking forward to it.

7. Polish your Crystal Ball.

In the 1939 classic, *The Wizard of Oz,* the distraught runaway, Dorothy, stumbles upon the curer of all ills, Professor Marvel. The wise professor, and erstwhile Wizard, convinces Dorothy through the use of his crystal ball that her Auntie Em is desperately trying to find Dorothy to keep her safe from the impending storm. By using his fortunetelling abilities, he convinces Dorothy to return home to safety right away.

What storms are in your customers' path that you are warning them about? How are you leading them to a safe harbor? How well are you preparing them for success in the future? Are you helping add to their "fortunes"?

Suppliers and vendors provide a good service or a good product. Strategic partner status is reserved for those who have an area of expertise or exceptional value that customers tap into for significant and long-term value. Great suppliers become **indispensable resources** to their customers. They are fortunetellers who are able to bring the future to the present for the mutual benefit of both parties.

What trends can you become aware of on a regular basis that might have profound impact either short term or long term on your customers' business? Make certain you are "tuned in to" issues that can positively or negatively influence your customers' success. If you are the proverbial "canary in the mine shaft" for them, they will turn to you again and again for support because of your informative value, which ultimately can be, in most cases, more important than the actual value of the product or service you deliver. Fortunes often rise or fall based on the timing of knowing things, so you can act before others do.

Postage increases or changes in mailing regulations might alter the direct marketing campaigns of your clients. Lumber prices can affect the construction of new homes. Interest rate increases or decreases can help or hurt the re-financing industry. Changes in household income can dramatically impact consumer spending on discretionary purchases of every kind. There are literally thousands of examples that are even more specific to a certain business or industry. Finding ways to keep your customers informed will keep you in such a strong position as to be virtually invulnerable to the overtures of the competition.

Know your customer's business. Know what is important to your customers' customers. Products and services are important but information is king. Read the tea leaves. Help your customers see the future and reap the rewards.

8. Celebrate the Relationship.

Business is serious stuff, often conducted by serious (grim) people. But despite computers and technology, it's still done between people. And people like to enjoy themselves. They want to have relationships. People love to find reasons to celebrate. Find ways to incorporate celebrations into your business relationships and watch them blossom into long-lasting friendships.

All things being equal, and even when they're much less than equal, buyers will always steer business to those sellers with whom they have the best relationship. On a personal note, make sure you are aware of and acknowledge things like:

- Birthdays
- Birth of Children
- Engagements / Marriage
- Wedding Anniversaries
- Graduation from educational programs
- Vacations – bon voyage notes or small gifts
- Purchase of a new home

- Purchase of a new car

On the professional level, congratulate your customers for:

- New jobs
- Promotions
- Retirements
- Professional awards
- Good publicity in the media
- Mergers or acquisitions with or of other companies
- Success within professional associations or civic organizations

One of the more successful and relevant strategies for cementing lasting business with customers that I have seen is to celebrate the anniversary of the beginning of the relationship. We all gravitate toward things that are fun and make us feel good. Reminding customers you have been around for a while is not a bad idea. Reminding them of the value they've received because of your presence over time is even better.

If the first order came on March 15th, make March 15th the anniversary between the parties and never let it pass without a celebration. Light the candles. Sing a song. Cut the cake.

9. Don't Tell too many Fish Stories.

I'm not a fisherman. I'm a golfer. Well, actually Tiger Woods is a golfer; I just like to play the game. But every fisherman I know has several stories about "the one that got away." They tell you how it was *this big* (usually gesturing excitedly with hands or other visual aids) and explain in many different (some painful, some funny) ways why they don't have any pictures with the "would have been a record" catch.

In business we all have stories about the customer who got away. Some have one or two they can talk about, some have more. Too many stories and you'll be in big trouble. And instead of moaning about the defections, a better strategy is to try to get them back. In fishing parlance, if they took the bait once, they may again. If you can get a second chance, this time set the hook a little better.

Several businesses that I know make boastful claims about all the new customers they bring on board. Keeping one customer for ten years is infinitely more valuable then adding ten new customers who only buy for one year. If you have found the right customers, do not take their hinting at leaving lightly or easily. Fight like crazy to maintain the business.

A quick study of your database and the buying trends of your customers should give you better-than-average insight into who may not be buying from you anymore. If, despite your best efforts, you lose a customer or two that you want back, take these steps.

1. <u>Try to conduct an exit interview</u>. Don't make excuses, but show the customer you are sincerely upset at losing their business. Closed-ended questions that elicit yes or no answers are of no value to you. Ask what, when, who, which, and how questions. Why questions may be viewed as too confrontational.

2. <u>Ask two final questions to close the interview</u>. Number one, "Is there something we can do right now to earn the business back?" If they give you a remedy you can live with, do it. It will be much easier to restart now instead of trying to win the business back after the competition has had it for some time. Number two, if the answer is no, get permission to "keep them on the list." If you can get them to agree to allow you to continue to market them, at least the door is still slightly ajar.

3. <u>Be extremely active and specific with your marketing effort to these "lost fish."</u> If you've done a good job on the exit interview you will

have gained substantial information about what is important to the customer and what may appeal to them in the future.

Although in many studies customers say they stop doing business with a company for no specific reason, don't believe it. Customers leave typically because you gave them a reason to with what you did, or did not, do. With the customers you want to keep, try to develop a zero tolerance of defections culture. Make it mission critical for every employee to understand the need to keep 'em--before they get away.

The TV is full of reality shows where contestants vie to be the last one standing to collect the big prize. Don't wake up to find yourself "voted off the island" by your customers. But if you do, build a raft, sail toward it, and try to get back on.

10. Where's the Wow?

For years now, on every 4th of July, we pack the kids in the family car and head off to the fireworks show at the local park. And while it is always entertaining, this past year we started whispering halfway through that maybe we would not come back next year. Been there, done that. Seen one, seen 'em all. Then, all of a sudden, it started. The mother of all finales. Explosions of color and sound all over the sky. It lasted for more than fifteen minutes. **Incredible!** Definitely worth going back for.

How many of your customers feel the same about your service? Even if it's good, is it enough? Is there a Wow factor, something unexpected that is worth coming back for? Remember the three possible outcomes of a customer interaction with your company. Expectations not met. We know what happens then. Expectations met. Do you really want only a 50/50 chance of retaining customers? Expectations exceeded. Now we're talking.

Now, one carload of kids, even mine, would not dramatically alter the economics of a community fireworks show. Sure, a few less glow-sticks, buckets of popcorn, lemonade and hotdogs would be sold, but the vendors would not go out of business. But multiply the not-coming-back effect slightly and it just may. Try losing 3 or 5 or 10 percent of your business because you provide only average value rather than something special and see what happens.

In this day and age of choice and global competition, deliver the basics and consumers are likely to judge you unfavorably. Deliver the basics along with what is expected and you might get a middle of the road rating. Only when you start to exceed expectations do customers begin to think about coming back on a regular basis.

Once you've been to Disney World it's sometimes hard to get excited about the local amusement park. Once you've seen the Grand Canyon the nearby scenic spots sometimes don't measure up. When you've flown 1st class a few times, coach can seem like 2nd class. Because it is.

Don't let your customers get more from the competition than they can get from you. Attention spans are short. Loyalty is fleeting. Give them the grand finale all the time. If you want to keep your customers, find something you can Wow 'em with. Now.

11. Six Things Not to Do.

When Moses came down the mountain with the Ten Commandments, God called them that because they were really not suggestions. Although there are many shades of grey in customer service, if I were to be bold, these would absolutely be the Six Don't Do Commandments of customer service.

1. <u>Don't Lie.</u> Some years ago I bought my first really nice car – a Cadillac. Wanting to do things right to take care of it, I decided to bring it back to the dealer for service. After the warranty had expired on many of the standard items covered, the electronic dashboard went blank suddenly. After having brought it in and being assured that I would receive a call in the morning I went away satisfied as to the concern and prompt response.

   The next day came and went, however, with no call. When I inquired the following day I was assured that the replacement had been ordered and they needed to keep the car only one more day. Calling at the end of the following business day I was told that the part was on back order and would be delayed. Dismayed I decided to visit the dealer the following day only to find out the car had not even been looked at yet. Frustrated about being lied to, I took the car elsewhere for service. And I drive an Acura now.

2. <u>Don't cheat</u>. When my wife and I began the family, we went looking to buy a nice, used minivan to help fulfill our duty as good subur-

ban parents. After looking at several choices, we spotted and test-drove a model we really liked.

Jumping in the car, the salesperson informed us the price was $12,900, very fair for the age and condition we thought. The test drive went well and we got out ready to buy. Upon seeing our excitement the salesperson quoted us a price of $13,900. Stunned, we said that he mentioned the price was $12,900 when we got in and how could it go up $1000 after a test drive. He tried to convince us he said $13,900 and we walked out. Trying to take advantage of your customers is no way to get them or keep them.

3. <u>Don't accuse.</u> It may seem like I'm picking on the car dealers but it's a true story. On still another vehicle purchase excursion, I decided to go with the dealer's financing company instead of my tried and true local bank.

    While understanding that we needed to pay the subsequent monthly bills on time, I became engaged in a six month battle with the financing company suggesting that it would be far easier to do if I got their statement before the actual due date, if I got one at all. After one particularly frustrating episode I asked to speak with a customer service manager to assure them that I was happy to pay, just looking for a little help. To which came the reply that my claims of mail not received on time or at all were, *"ridiculous and that I was obviously lying."* To which my reply was to re-finance with my local bank and pay off the loan.

4. <u>Don't try to cover-up mistakes.</u> When renovating the house on one occasion, we picked what we thought would be a very nice and functional carpet for the family room, which was the first area to be done. When I came home the day of the installation to find ¾ inch seams running throughout the room I was a little upset. No problem my wife said, she had called and someone would be there the next day.

    The call from my wife the next day was not quite as pleasant. The person who had come out to review the job assured my wife that the seams would "come together" after walking on the carpet for a little while. Much more annoyed than amused, a second inspector came out the following day and said the job would be replaced but that we shouldn't have ordered that kind of carpet for a room that needed that many cuts (despite the fact their person came to measure and review the job). Our fault, I guess. They did not get the other eight rooms we carpeted during that renovation.

5. <u>Don't criticize your own company.</u> We recently had a service repairperson come and fix   some appliances. He called on the way to the appointment to ask me for directions and to learn what the problem was. But the conversation was mostly about how "they" always sent him out without knowing what he was supposed to do.

At the appointment, he continued to "pan" his company. He mentioned how he dealt with these kinds of problems over and over again. He could not understand how, despite being a **major** corporation, they just could not engineer good products. He elaborated, at length, how the advertising was all lies. The topper was when he asked if I was interested in buying an extended warranty program at the end of the repair! Suffice it to say which brand I *will not* be buying next time.

6. <u>If you don't make it easy to buy.</u> If you don't take credit cards, you're missing out on sales. Don't offer automatic checking account payments. You're shortchanging yourself. Need to "fill out forms" to make a sale? Forget about it. Don't have online access to place orders. You're in trouble. Your competitors have already, or will, figure out ways that your customers can do these things with them if you don't find a way to do so.

No trust – no sale. No convenience – no sale. Make it easy for the customer to buy orsomeone else will.

12. The Good, the Bad, and the Ugly.

People love to talk. Not everyone. And not all the time. But in general, people search for material for conversations with friends, co-workers, families and acquaintances. And people love to share stories about how they were *treated*, better or worse, good or bad, fairly or unfairly. Their sharing about customer service experiences they've had with your organization, the word-of-mouth, could make or break your business over time.

Your reputation is on the line every time you pick up the phone, have someone walk in the door, check out your marketing material and make a purchase. Do you know what the prospect or customer thinks or says after the transaction? Despite the improvements gained by sophisticated technology, when humans and computers and machines are involved, there will always be things that don't go exactly quite right.

How you handle a problem when one arises is almost always more important than the fact that one came up in the first place. Most people don't expect perfection, but they do expect satisfaction if they've invested time, effort and money to buy your product. Holding up signs like "it's company policy" or offering cumbersome processes to rectify a complaint are surefire ways to lose that customer, and perhaps, many more as well.

In the sales training classes that we ran for some time for our new salespeople, we used to give them a very specific homework assignment on the first day. We sent them home and asked them (in this order) to give us the best and worst customer service experience that they could remember. When they came in to discuss the homework the following day, we always asked, again in the same order, for their best and worst experience. Do you know what happened? Despite asking (twice) for the best first and the worst second, 19 of the 21 people we trained during those few years came back with their worst experience first. **90%!**

And not only that, the stories of woe were much longer, much more emotional and more vivid than the good experiences. Asked if they continued to buy from the company that had annoyed them so much, only three said that the problem got handled well enough for them to continue being a customer. Sixteen voted with their feet and took their business elsewhere.

Many studies have been taken over time around this phenomenon. What I've seen still indicates that a happy customer might tell three people if something went right while an unhappy customer probably will tell sixteen people. The odds are not in your favor if you're not making people happy. Hopefully most people are more than satisfied with the majority of the interactions they have with you. But if not, move to make 'em happy – fast.

13. How much is a Thank You worth?

At the end of the last chapter we talked about sincerely thanking your new customer with a note, gift or some sort of acknowledgement of appreciation for the business. But what is the real value of the "touchy feely" stuff you might ask?

My favorite example of this is actually one that is different from the first three I mentioned. Once when both my wife and I were trying to get on one of the early healthy eating trends, we cashed in an offer from a health food company for returning five box tops for a $5 rebate. When the $5 check came in the mail, with it was a very nice, personalized, handwritten note thanking us for the purchases, hoping that we would continue to enjoy their products and wishing us "good health." The product was good but the attention was great. The note is still saved in a file with some of the most memorable customer service examples received over the last twenty years.

I've estimated that we've purchased two boxes of this company's cereal a week ($6.00). And one container of shake mix ($14.00). And the occasional box of cereal bars or other "treats" ($5.00).

That's only $35.00 per week. But it's $140.00 per month. And it's $1680.00 per year. **Over twenty years, that is approximately $33,600!** That two minute, handwritten note, $5.00 rebate and whatever-cents stamp that the company invested earned them more than $30,000 over twenty years. Now if the product was no good or my tastes changed over time the result would surely be different. But the note created a *better chance* to build the long-term relationship.

Commonly referred to as the "lifetime value" of a customer, the realization of this principle will change your day-to-day behaviors and long-term strategy. It will help you more accurately deploy resources today and predict where more might be needed in the future.

Consider these nine points to help determine the lifetime value of your relationship with each customer:

1. Average annual revenue of the customer.
2. Average value of returns – if any.
3. Length of time an average customer stays with you.
4. Calculate the gross margin from this customer.
5. Average dollar increase in business from the customer.

6. How much (if any) your marketing or advertising expense goes down because of not needing to reach out to this customer.

7. The average dollar value of business that the customer refers to you.

8. Any increase in margin due to increased value over time.

9. Any technological impact, pro or con, that will enhance or diminish your product and service revenue over time.

Saying thank you is the polite thing to do, just like Mom taught you. And it just so happens to also equal lots of $$$'s.

14. Put your money where your mouth is.

So you've come up with a new slogan. "Our customers are #1." Fabulous. Or even better, "customer service is our top priority." Brilliant. But how come you don't put your money where your mouth is? Why are your frontline customer service people only a pay grade ahead of minimum wage? Your customers are your most valuable asset. Why do so many organizations settle for "average" performers in the vital position of customer contact agents? Maybe fast food restaurants can get away with it, but not companies where there is more competition and choices for consumers.

One of the best ways to keep the right customers over the long haul is to attract, acquire and retain the best (right) customer service help. Average performers will perform averagely. Only superior performers will take care of the customer in a way that will make them want to come back to you again and again. The more successful companies have always, currently do, and in the future will find the most talented employees and put them in positions of responsibility taking care of the customer. Better people make better business, and a better bottom line.

Ongoing demographic shifts will make this issue more challenging than in the past. Workforce diversity will only continue to rise. Geography and population shifts also play a part. A dearth of younger experienced workers and a glut of older workers wanting to remain at least partly active in the workforce will force you to consider new ways to hire, train and deploy customer service specialists. Issues you may look at include:

<u>Home-based work force.</u> Many organizations that employ higher quality workers are able to cut overhead by eliminating central offices. Technology makes this

easier every day. Productivity increases can be related back to:

- Being able to work at personal peak efficiency times
- Fewer days missed due to family or incidental reasons
- A more flexible work schedule
- Less difficulties with commuting
- More freedom from office politics
- Much fewer interruptions, meetings and other distractions

Commission-based pay plans. If it is good for your salespeople, then it is OK for your customer service specialists as well. Tie pay to performance with sales volume, profit or retention metrics.

Less command and control management. Higher quality and older workers will have far different needs, expectations, values and experiences than people you may have hired in the past. Flexibility and participation in the decision-making process will be a must.

The ideal customer service specialists are problem-solvers that have excellent interpersonal communication skills, are technologically savvy, and are motivated self-starters. They can plan and execute their own work under minimal supervision. They are able to learn quickly, adapt to change and think creatively. In short, they are "A" players. Don't settle for "B" or "C" unless you want a "B" or "C" result.

There's no mystery that in sports the teams that are able to spend the most on players usually make the playoffs. The Boston Red Sox and New York Yankees spend more money on one or two players than some organizations do on their entire team. They buy "A" players. Not that the best players always come together to make the best *team*. That takes coaching, intangibles and an element of luck. But having the most talent is not a bad place to start.

To keep customers long term you are asking them to make an investment in you. Give them one back. Put your "skin in the game." Hire the best people you can find to take care of your biggest asset--your customers.

15. Keep 'Em Coming Back

Loyalty: Look up synonyms and you'll find words like: faithfulness, allegiance, devotion, constancy, fidelity and dependability. The word loyal has words like trustworthy, steadfast, stable, reliable, unwavering and reliable attached to it. More than just words, these are the cornerstone concepts and philosophies that make for great relationships between friends, families, communities and even nations. And yes, businesses.

A breakdown in loyalty on either side of a relationship begins to make it one-sided. And although one-way signs are OK for certain road conditions, it makes for poor partnerships in any area, including business. The only way to Keep 'Em coming back in the long run is to maintain loyalty on both sides of the relationship. And the onus is on you.

The customer for their part has to choose to do what's best for their particular situation. It's up to you to make sure you have the right answers for each individual customer. Initiate a formal retention and recognition program that is appropriate for your business and your customers. Loyalty begins with your efforts to foster it and maintain it. Consider the following eight suggestions to improve the likelihood of the customers you have, the right customers, coming back.

1. Accountability: Consider giving your customer service people higher levels of responsibility for customer satisfaction. Where possible, play "finder's keepers." The person who discovers the customer's problem is the one who

solves the customer's problem. People do not like to be "passed along." At Hilton Hotels, employees have wide latitude to solve a customer issue or complaint, including a healthy budget.

2. <u>Focus on the customer</u>: Managers of all kinds are often overwhelmed with internal concerns and distractions. Software updates and computer problems. Reports. Employee issues of all kinds. These problems take the focus off where it should be, the customer. Is 80 percent of your time directed toward customer requirements and only 20 percent toward internal issues? If not, your time is misspent. By paying attention to what the customer needs, you'll be paying attention to what your organization needs as well.

3. <u>Stay close to the customer</u>: Perform a SWOT (Strengths, Weaknesses, Opportunities, Threats) analysis on each customer on a regular basis. Ask questions like:

- Why does this customer buy from us?
- How well do we meet their requirements and expectations?
- What can we do to be more valuable to them?

- What issues or problems have we had with them lately?
- How do they think we positively impact their business?
- Are we considered a vendor or a partner?
- How do they view the competition?
- How strong is our relationship and at what level?
- What may change in the future that will impact the relationship?
- What things must we avoid doing in order to not lose the business?
- How will/can technology change things now or in the future?

4. <u>Create a suggestion program</u>. Offer your customers an easy way to give you suggestions about the value of your products and services rendered to them and how to improve in the future. Use the feedback to spot trends and make course corrections in your strategy and execution.

5. <u>Encourage complaints</u>. Don't sweep them under the rug. Odds are, if you hear about an issue that one customer is having, others may be experiencing it as well. The tip of the iceberg may not hurt you much but it was the stuff

underneath the water that sank the Titanic.

6. <u>Be proactive</u>. Nordstrom, the gold standard of customer service, encourages their sales/customer service employees to know all there is to know about their individual clients. When certain clothing items come into a store, associates may "match up" an item with a certain customer based on style preferences and previous buying habits. They will call the customer to say they have found something special for them and will hold it until they can come down to have "first crack" at it.

7. <u>Give 'em more than they expect</u>. Whether very rigidly crafted or randomly, make sure you surprise and delight your customers with more than they expect on a regular basis. Sometimes it can be a little thing or sometimes a big thing, depending on the circumstances. Throw an extra bagel in the bag. Give them something free every 5th or 10th or whatever visit. Don't give them any reason to think the competition would treat them better than you.

8. <u>Help them become advocates.</u> A loyal customer is one that comes back. An ultra-loyal customer is one that comes back **and** helps you recruit new business partners as well. At the end of the day, your loyal, satisfied

customers, the testimonials, references and enthusiasm they bring because of the relationship they have with you, is more valuable than an unlimited marketing budget chasing prospects who don't know you.

9. <u>Help them sell the product you sold them</u>. One medical device manufacturer I know offers buyers of their device a turnkey marketing process including advertising purchases in different media and direct mail campaigns to key influencers. Increasing demand from end users is a wonderful way to create pull-through for your product or service.

10. <u>Practice the magic words and phrases</u>. Please, thank you and you're welcome are a good start. Try adding, "how may we help?" "sure," "no problem," "I don't know but I'll find out," and "yes, we can" to your vocabulary. They are music to your customer's ears.

In the final analysis, your customer must become a partner in your success by your becoming one in theirs. Loyalty and repeat business is earned through the spirit of mutual cooperation in achieving the customers' goals.

Old joke. "What do you call a boomerang that doesn't come back?" Answer. "A stick." You want your customers to be boomerangs, not sticks. It takes precise craftsmanship and engineering to turn a stick or piece of wood into a high functioning boomerang that performs as expected and comes back every time. Placing your customers at the very center of all of your thinking, planning, systems, training, strategy and execution is the very best way to make them want to be boomerangs and return to you again and again and again.........

Epilogue

A Lesson from Nature – The Venus Flytrap

The Venus Flytrap is nature's equivalent of a well-run marketing, sales and retention program. Like many plants they get fed both from gases in the air and nutrients in the soil. But it is in catching the "right" insects that the flytrap will truly thrive rather than just exist. To be considered carnivorous, a plant must *attract, capture* and *digest* some kind of animal life.

The plant must first secrete a sweet-smelling sap that is attractive to its intended prey (marketing). After an insect lands on the plant's trap it will close in about one second, but not all the way. Insects that are too small or too large are released because they provide inadequate nutrition or are "too big to swallow"(sales qualification). Stones, nuts or other inadvertent objects are released in about twelve hours if they don't meet the flytrap's expectations (firing the wrong customers). If the plant finds the captive bug to its' liking however, (the "just right" customer), the trap is shut tight, never to open again until the next catch (retention).

Things in nature usually work very well. Design your marketing, sales and retention process just as well to achieve long-term success and restful nights.

Glossary of Terms

KBF – <u>Key Buying Factors.</u> The unique "hot buttons" or circumstances that are the most important conditions for each individual buyer when considering a purchase.

DMS – <u>Decision Making System</u>. The process that a prospect or customer will go through to make a buy / no buy decision.

PLC – <u>Perceived Level of Credibility</u>. Each customer's perception of your company as a viable option with whom to do business.

ATI – <u>Ability to Influence</u>. The strength of your position with each prospect when they are close to making a buying decision.

MLB – <u>Most Likely to Buy</u>. Those prospects or customers that see the greatest value in your product or service offering.

CPC – <u>Critical Points of Contact</u>. The interactions or specific communications that occur during a buying cycle.

About the Author

Brian Butler is vice president of business development for The Allied Group, a leading provider of both sophisticated kitting & fulfillment services and high impact marketing communications and lead generation programs for the life science, higher education and financial services industries.

In his speaking and training capacity, Brian has given numerous keynote addresses and presentations for organizations such as AARP Services Inc., IBM, The American Yacht Charter Association, Atlas Travel International and One Communications.

Brian holds a BS in marketing, graduating with honors from the University of Bridgeport, where he attended school on a two-sport athletic scholarship for soccer and baseball. He also earned an MBA from Century University. Currently, he lives in East Greenwich, Rhode Island.